ENDURANCE EXECUTIVE

Lisa,

Thank you for all your support in our establishing my new group.

ENDURANCE EXECUTIVE

A CEO's Perspective on the Marathon of Elite Business Performance

ALEX P. BARTHOLOMAUS

ISBN: 0996935606
ISBN 13: 9780996935609

DEDICATION

To my wife Mary, and our 3 beautiful children Lily, Jack and Leo. You all inspire me to be my best and I thank you for all of your love, encouragement and support.

TABLE OF CONTENTS

INTRODUCTION

In 2001, I was a busy entrepreneur and family man, responsible for the health and welfare of both my business and my wife and children. Feeling a need to nurture both my body and mind, I took an interest in running. It proved to be a great outlet that strengthened my body, and began to shape my life, mind, and worldview in ways I never thought possible.

It wasn't long until my passion for running transformed into a new goal: I wanted to complete a marathon. It was difficult to find time to train, given a hectic travel schedule, family commitments, and a growing business. Around this same time, I exited my first business and started to build a consulting company. This venture freed me up and allowed me to focus again on my marathon goal.

As fate should have it, a little too much training produced an injury that sidetracked my efforts, but my consulting business took off. The harder I worked, and the more I learned about endurance sports, the more parallels I drew between the struggles of marathoners who "hit the wall," and those of the successful executives I've come into contact with in my own professional life.

The wall is a term runners use to describe the point at which your body is no longer able to process the lactic acid produced by your muscles during extreme exertion. This leads to intense pain and cramping in the feet, calves, quads, glutes, hips, and back. Your focus suffers, and your sense of determination falters. My clients suffer the same fate, except instead of a road race, it's the race to become successful and/or attain new levels of success.

As these leaders and senior executives pursue more challenging goals and bigger accomplishments, most will encounter a period where it feels they hit the wall. Career overexertion often has devastating consequences. In other cases, the wall can be a long career plateau, a feeling of stagnation that can't be easily overcome. When this plateau or stagnant period is not addressed, executives eventually start to experience a slow decline in work success and personal happiness.

Thankfully, just as athletes are able to endure the physical challenges of a race to reach the finish line, the successful professional with the right mindset and toolkit, can evolve into an "Endurance Executive." Endurance Executives are high-achieving and long-lasting in their careers. Most of us will hit the wall at some point, but how we respond is the key to long-term professional success.

This book addresses my personal endurance story—how I responded in the Marine Corp marathon—and the key concepts that I learned while participating. The experience acted as a catalyst to help me build an Endurance Executive mindset and approach to work and life. I have successfully used this approach to help the clients in my consulting business perform at a greater level and avoid the wall.

THE MARATHON

The Marine Corps Marathon in Washington DC is one of the largest marathons in the world, with over 40,000 participants. I was lucky enough to be able to participate in October of 2013. I followed a training program to prepare, and my goal was to finish in less than four hours. I was a member of a local running group, and a bunch of us ran in the marathon together, so I felt that I had the support of a strong team. When I started the marathon, it was pure jubilation; the energy of the race was incredible. You run up a hill on Old Lee Highway and then down Spout Run Parkway, before getting to the Key Bridge.

I crossed into Georgetown, and ran up Rock Creek Parkway. At Kennedy Center, around mile nine, a weird thing happened. I don't know what made me think of my departed mother but I did, and almost started hyperventilating. I told myself, "Keep it together, you're running a great race." This self-talk allowed me to keep my focus, but I let off the pedal when I realized I started out fast. While my twelfth and thirteenth miles were at a slower pace, I still hit my mid-race goal of under two hours.

I arrived at mile 14 and my feet felt great, but suddenly my quad tightened up, causing pain to emanate into my back. Thirty seconds later, that same pain hit the other leg, so with each step I took, searing pain shot through my legs and back. I vividly recall looking at my watch, which indicated I'd crossed the 14-mile mark, when the first of the painful cramps sets into my quads. I thought, "Oh my God that hurts so much. This can't be happening to me. I have 12 miles to go. What am I going to do?"

When you hit the wall, you wonder how you will keep moving, because the pain is overwhelming. Yet, the inner voice steps in to guide your direction, so in spite of the pain an athlete perseveres. I never bothered to ask myself, "Why?" I just kept on going.

TOO FAR, TOO FAST

When the cramps set in, my legs felt as if they weighed a hundred pounds each, with both quads in full spasm. I slowed down, tried to calm my breathing, and realized I was hitting the wall. A sinking feeling of despair struck me, as I had mentally prepared for hitting the wall at mile 20, 21 or 22. At the end of the race, in that late stage, I could have pushed through and gutted out the last four or six miles.

Instead, I had 12 remaining miles, about two to three times more distance than I expected. I thought, "Okay, I've got to pull it together. I have to hang in there. I can't stop." I had to figure out what I needed to do to finish. The next mile or two was about putting one foot in front of the other, regaining my composure, and just trying to make it to the finish line.

I didn't want to hyperventilate, so I focused on my breathing and on keeping my stride lengths short to conserve energy. I asked myself "Okay, how long before I stop and stretch? The only way I'm going to get through is by stopping, stretching, and running." Around the fifteenth mile, I had my first stop and I stretched both quads. I don't know if it was 30 seconds or 60 seconds, but it provided amazing relief from a crescendo of pain. Then I was off again, into a slow jog. When my nine-minute mile pace had slowed to 11 minutes, I knew I'd gone into survival mode and that there was no way I was hitting my four hour goal. I thought, "Okay, the only way I'm going to do this is if I just try to do it a mile at a time. When the pain crescendos, I'm either going to stop when I have to stop, or stop every mile, stretch, and continue."

I began looking at people, and drawing energy from the crowd. It gave me encouragement. They could see that I was struggling, and offered their encouragement to me (and the rest of the runners)—unconditionally. One of the key factors that will help you avoid the wall is to pace yourself and nourish your body over the course of the race. The function of the wall is to stop you when your body has run out of energy, when it's overwhelmed.

I used my determination, my willpower, my refusal to accept defeat, as a means of creating a plan that allowed me to get through the race. It wasn't my ideal situation, but when you hit the wall—either in sports or business—having a strong focus and a plan to break past the wall will rescue you from failure.

RESPONDING TO THE WALL

We don't have as much control over our bodies as most of us would like. Some of us entrepreneurs, who invest a tremendous amount of time and energy into our work, may also lose a sense of control over our personal lives, our families, and what we value most.

When a runner hits the wall, he or she must be able to evaluate the situation to make responsible, safe, and self-aware choices that will replenish the body's energy and allow that person to continue toward the finish line. The hard work and "endurance" mindset of a successful businessperson often mirrors that of a successful athlete. Rather than accepting defeat, when an advanced career professional hits the wall at work, they must step back and establish how to best recover, in a way that will allow them to quickly rejoin the race.

During my time in business and sports, I have seen striking similarities in the positive recovery choices made by both athletes and hardworking professionals in all occupations. These include reflection and intrapersonal awareness; focused commitment to goals; building a strong support system at work and at home; taking care of one's mind and body; and preparation to ready the body and mind for enduring periods of intense stress. By utilizing all of these tactics, a work+life balance can be achieved, promoting well-rounded development of character, and long-term professional success.

Learning to deal with hitting the wall requires building a specific mindset. All experienced professionals have unique ways of breaking through the wall, and integrate these tactics into their daily lives in a systematic way that prevents long-term breakdown and burnout.

AN END IN SIGHT

Slowly but surely, I got to the sixteenth mile. It was amazing to see the number of people who came out to the Marine Corps Marathon, all cheering for the runners. When runners hit the wall during a race, they can rely on the support and encouragement of those cheering onlookers to get them through the ordeal and back on track. In my own experience racing, I felt deeply motivated not to let my family down, because like the others lining the racecourse, they were extremely supportive.

When you're going through such a painful experience, there are many circumstances and ideas on which to reflect. Both runners and business professionals find themselves asking, "What could I, or should I, have done to avoid this situation?" My job involved working with CEO's and teams who experience a metaphorical wall, so it seemed ironic that here I was—the person who's always advising others how to avoid or get past it, experiencing my own wall at the most inopportune time. We all have moments where it feels that our bodies and minds simply cannot go on; no one is completely immune to hitting the wall.

For some people, it's more like slamming full-force into the wall. Suddenly, they find themselves in a state of extreme mental or physical agony, such as depression, substance abuse or poor health. For others, more subtle, persistent feelings of discomfort slowly reveal that they've reached a tipping point, and must reassess certain lifestyle choices in order to recover and get back on track. When the pain is less acute, not searing, it takes people longer to become aware of the wall.

Professionally, people's careers typically plateau when they hit the wall, though sometimes they can lose traction and start on a downward slide. When we look at these career plateaus, we try to:

1. Help people understand that they have hit the wall
2. Help them understand what the wall means
3. Help them learn how to work through the current situation
4. Give them skills to prevent future recurrences

Sometimes, at work, people hit the wall and they don't realize it. By comparison, hitting the wall in a marathon is always an obvious experience. When I compare the types of people who hit the wall in their careers—whether it's a CEO, a VP or a salesperson—they all come from different backgrounds. They have many different goals and can hit the wall for a variety of different reasons. Regardless of why, self awareness is critical to both realizing one has reached this point, and to maintaining composure. In the middle of the race, a runner doesn't have the luxury of time, and must work hard to compose him or herself quickly. In work life, we have days, weeks and months to work through our struggles and make it to the finish line.

It's easy for ambitious people to hit the wall, especially if they go after their goals in a reckless manner. Ambitious executives pursue their objectives without being as mindful of the potential consequences of running too far, too fast. That's what happened to me out there. I was like any other executive going for a big promotion or a big sale, only to find myself in the middle of a race, having already hit the wall, with many miles left to go.

THE JOURNEY

Imagine that you have become aware you've hit the wall, and now it is time to think about where you really want to go. The process of becoming more self-aware and seeing your value systems mature is a type of journey. During my race, when the pain was nearly unbearable, I thought about my past and the journey I'd taken that led me to this particular point. I used these thoughts to distract myself from the discomfort. I reflected back to the point two years after my mom's death when the haze from her passing had lifted. I vividly recalled being on a trip to New Zealand with two colleagues. It was an adventure, my first time in New Zealand, and when I came back I was invigorated to take over the world with my wine business. I was ready to grow as a human being, a professional, and a father and husband.

To go far in your journey requires the consistent pursuits of self-actualization and knowledge. I've chosen to pursue knowledge for the betterment of my business. I could see our growth slowing after many years of expansion, and I knew that if I didn't learn more about human beings on a deeper level, it would potentially hold us back from growing more. I immersed myself in learning about psychology and behavioral science.

My desire to learn more coincided with my son Jack's diagnosis of PDDNOS (Pervasive Development Disorder Not Otherwise Specified) at the end of 2002. Any boy or girl suspected to be on the autism spectrum is diagnosed with the PDDNOS label before they refer to the child as autistic. This allows for testing and time to confirm that the diagnosis really is autism. My wife and I were motivated by Jack's condition to seek knowledge. We read books and articles, so that we could better understand and care for the needs of our child.

The increased push to learn allowed me to gain great insight into the way the human mind works. The research we did for Jack, on top of what I read about psychology and behavioral science for white collar performance at work, expanded my knowledge base and helped me grow as a person. As I gained more knowledge, my company began to expand once again. Thanks to all my reading and new understanding of neuroscience, psychology, and behavioral science, I was able to influence and mentor people in a positive way. My investment in building their self-awareness and skill sets helped them to perform better, driving new levels of growth for their companies and mine as well.

PASSION, DESIRE, AND COMMITMENT: MOTIVATIONAL FUEL FOR THE JOURNEY

At mile 17, when I composed myself and regained some rhythm in my stride, I knew I needed to think about things that would motivate me to persevere through the wall I had just hit. I began to think about my loved ones, and how they had endured serious challenges in their lives. I thought about my mom's eight-year battle with cancer. I thought about my 14-year-old son, Jack, who has special needs, and how hard my wife and I worked to provide him with a loving home. My wife raised Jack and two other children while I traveled for work. Her investment in our children has been incredible.

The struggles of my mother, wife, and son are real, and they made me realize, "I can do this. My mom did it; Jack lives with it every day, I can absolutely do this." It may be a cliché, but what doesn't kill you really does make you stronger. We have all gone through different challenges in our lives, but our stories of perseverance can inspire success in others. Motivation is a key part of our journey, as business leaders and as human beings. While struggling through the Marine Corps race, I had time on my hands to explore what it means to stay motivated and it helped me get through the painful experience.

I believe that my passion is a significant part of what has made my life successful and fulfilling. A great example of passion has been my commitment to achieving excellence in a focused area like business. After my mom passed away in 2000, the next two years of my life were a blur. I barely remember anything from 2001, except for 9/11. At the end of 2002, the haze started lifting and one of the things I knew I was passionate about was being the best, and making other people into better versions of themselves. This period kicked off some amazing growth for my last company as we grew from $15 million in revenue to $37 million in five years, while focusing on excellence as one of our core values.

I thought about, and took inspiration from, all of my passions. I worked in the wine business for over 15 years; even in that industry, where the product is amazing, over time it can be hard to feel genuine passion for a product when it's your job to sell it. Since I've been working in consulting and not full-time in the wine business, I have reached a wonderful place in my life where I can be more passionate about wine itself.

My family is passionate about hiking. I'm passionate about creating and growing my business. I'm an entrepreneur at heart and that passion for business is why I so enjoy what I do professionally. I'm extremely passionate about helping people grow.

Drawing inspiration from our passions allows us to use another important emotion, desire, as a means of bringing into focus what we wish to accomplish. When we desire a new car, a title, an academic credential, or a promotion at work, that sense of wanting allows us to envision a specific objective or outcome to work toward. Desire gives us something to work for, and when we have a detailed image of what that looks like, we're better able to conceptualize a plan for getting there.

Oftentimes, people blur the lines between desire and commitment, but desire is the specific thing that we want, while commitment is the effort one is willing to put forth in order to obtain it. During my race, I made a commitment to walk as little as possible, and do everything within my power to run a respectable time.

Frequently, when we look critically at people's professional and personal lives, commitment is where they fall short. This is because they make conditional commitments. If everything does not go exactly according to the perfect plans they have constructed in their minds, the commitment suddenly seems less important. Serious commitment requires serious investment of emotional and physical energy. Sure, I would have loved to run a race without both of my quads cramping every mile, but I didn't have a choice. I could have stopped, walked, and rationalized, "Now that I'm not going to make a perfect time anymore, why try?" I didn't give myself the luxury of copping out by using that excuse. I decided to put forth every ounce of effort to persevere and show my commitment to the goal of finishing the race and making my loved ones proud.

GOALS: PERSONAL, FAMILY, AND PROFESSIONAL

At one point in the race, I thought about my marathon goal. Had I set a realistic one for my first marathon? Had I thought about how it impacted other parts of my life? Our lives are divided into several interconnected aspects: personal life, family, and our professional lives. People who attain an initial level of success, then run into challenges, do so because as their lives become more demanding, and they fail to consider the complexity of each of these categories and how one affects all the others. People who hit the wall have often lost sight of their goals in one or more of these areas.

When it comes to the worlds of personal and family life versus professional life, many companies try to separate these or encourage employees to compartmentalize. We have all heard the clichés: "Don't take work home with you," and "Keep your work and home life separate." But that's really hard to do and might be an unrealistic expectation. At my last company, we tried to focus on developing people professionally, but we knew and acknowledged openly that developing them professionally would affect them positively in their family and personal lives as well.

I have made a lot of headway in my personal journey over the last five years—towards the end of selling my first company and starting my current company—by paying close attention to managing my personal, family, and professional goals, and making sure that the objectives I have for each area of my life are congruent. It can be nearly impossible to achieve a perfect balance, which is why I focus on alignment and congruency as more attainable than balancing all three.

Unfortunately, people cannot always assign the same amount of time to each category, all at once. Sometimes, our families take precedence over our work obligations. Sometimes, work responsibilities are more pressing and urgent than attending a family event. Instead of seeking perfect balance, we must ask ourselves, "Am I spending enough time with my family so they are still getting enough support?" or "Am I spending enough time at work that my business is growing?"

BUILDING YOUR SUPPORT TEAM

I also learned from the Marine Corps marathon that I didn't have the right support team. Every leader needs to have a support team that will give feedback, encouragement, and hold other team members accountable. The support team can include colleagues, executive coaches, past mentors, friends, and family. After 2003, I was lucky to have developed my own board of advisors. That was the first iteration of my support team. I also had a peer executive forum from 2004 to 2007, so those were my two mechanisms that provided me amazing support.

I credit the support from my family, board of advisors, and my peer executive forum for driving the success of my company from 2004-2007. Even after the first peer executive forum disbanded, we all stayed friends. It was the trajectory of everyone's companies that caused us to disband, but our personal relationships evolved as a result of the shift.

When I started my new business in 2010, I started over with my support team. I only had my family and some advisors supporting me. Over the last four years, I have developed a new board of advisors that is as good—or better—than what I had originally. I don't have a peer executive group like before, but I have put together something similar, working with peers in my industry to collaborate on content and hold each other accountable to hit each person's goals. We meet monthly, but in some cases talk more frequently, which has been a huge help in growing my new business.

FOUR TYPES OF PREPARATION: PHYSICAL, EMOTIONAL, MENTAL, AND GOAL-SPECIFIC

After reflecting on the marathon experience from prep to race, I came to the conclusion that I had fallen short in terms of preparedness. When I tried to break it down where I fell short, I separated it into four categories: physical, emotional, mental, and goal-specific.

Physical Preparation: When it came to physical preparation, I did a great job of logging miles. A key aspect of taking care of your body, whether you are asking it to run a lot of miles or work a lot of hours, is the pace at which you push yourself. This is where I failed; I didn't run slow enough on my endurance runs to build enough endurance. In hindsight, it I had to ask myself, "Okay, those factors are really important, so why didn't I listen to my instincts?"

Emotional Preparation: This is where the emotional piece comes in, as my overconfidence was the problem. It requires immense self-awareness to overcome the potential pitfalls of being overconfident. Hitting the wall is extremely humbling. I'm happy I hit the wall, because it served as a learning experience. Now, when I look at achieving something, I'm more conservative and realistic about what I can and can't do, and what I need to do to increase my probability of success.

Oftentimes, preparation is about emotionally being in the right head-space. After the race, I asked, "Was my self-awareness where it needed to be? Was my discipline where it needed to be? Did I make excuses?" Yes, I was making excuses to myself by believing I could run a fast marathon weighing 193 pounds, rather than 180 or 175. I wasn't emotionally prepared to accept the fact that I was too heavy to race my best time.

Self-talk is another type of preparation that can keep you going after you've hit the wall. Even through the sinking feeling of despair, you can find a voice inside of you that says, "No, you can't quit." Everyone has that inner voice that talks to them at these times. Some people can have conflicting inner voices that present two options: stop, or go on. In my case, it was fairly easy. Outside of the race, when faced with daily life choices, sometimes there are several options for people to choose from. Quitting is an option, but for me it wasn't. In that regard, I was prepared emotionally for endurance, even when the going got rough.

The Endurance mindset is about not accepting defeat and instead focusing on preparing your emotions for good decision-making under fire. We ask ourselves questions such as, "Okay, what can I do? What do I have to do? What is the most important thing to do in the next 30 seconds, minute, five minutes?" The same applies when someone becomes aware of a career plateau. What are they doing that day, that week, that month that will allow them to start moving upwards again?

These are the key features of emotional preparation. Emotional preparation for any type of race or journey is different for each individual, and I saw this when growing my last business. These days, when I work with employees and clients, I focus on emotional intelligence—how I can better develop it in other people. People who are emotionally prepared look inward for the answers.

Goal-Specific Preparation: Every ambitious goal needs preparation that is specific to that goal. In my case, I was trying to run a marathon in under four hours, but I did not lose enough weight to give myself the best chance to run the fastest race. For a person of my height, I probably should have lost another ten pounds, so that was a criteria for success where I overestimated my capacity as an athlete.

Mental Preparation: I think mental preparation is fundamental because first you need to develop a strategy and then you have to stick to that strategy. I was mentally prepared to be aggressive. I probably ended up being more aggressive than I needed to be, so even though I thought I was mentally prepared, clearly it was not enough. Thanks to my mental fortitude, I was able to persevere, so while there was some mental preparation that did help me, there were still gaps where I fell short. I was too aggressive, and started the race at a faster than normal pace. A lack of mental preparation can hold people back from executing their best work or running their fastest, because they don't allow enough time to mentally prepare for their respective race or journey.

I had roughly two hours and 30 minutes to limp the last 12 miles. That gave me a lot of time to reflect. One of the key things to keep in mind about reflection, whether it's a few seconds, minutes, or more time, is that with our busy lives, most of us only have the mental bandwidth to reflect on a couple of things at one time. If we reflect at the end of the day, it's better than nothing, but during that brief period of time you should focus on what is most important to you.

Many times in the morning as I'm going to work, I'll reflect on what's important to my family. Those interactions are fresh in my mind, because we just had breakfast and we were all together, talking to one another. When I reflect, I want to consider the moment that I just experienced with the people who matter to me.

During these quiet moments, the main question I ask myself is, "Am I being the best person that I can be? How can I improve on that? How can I be a better father for my children? How can I be a better husband? How can I be a better boss? I consider whether I've done a good job in all of these areas because if I'm satisfied with that particular area of my life—at least for the moment—then I can move onto considering the next concern.

I credit the fair amount of time I spend on reflection and thinking for helping with the growth of my businesses. The nice thing about running is that I get a chance to think about important things in my life. Often, running time becomes business problem-solving time. I also reflect when I'm lying in bed or meditating—it's important to find time to rest and let your thoughts wander—but there's something special about doing it when I run. Thinking allows your body to regenerate from a rest perspective, but it also allows your mind to reflect on what is important.

The marathon experience, while painful, proved pivotal in helping me articulate a mindset that I had been trying to live by and teach to my clients. In this book, we will explore the primary elements of this mindset and approach, to help leaders and senior executives get past the wall—or avoid it altogether. We will build a skill set and worldview that nurtures people toward greater levels of success and personal happiness, both in the workplace and at home.

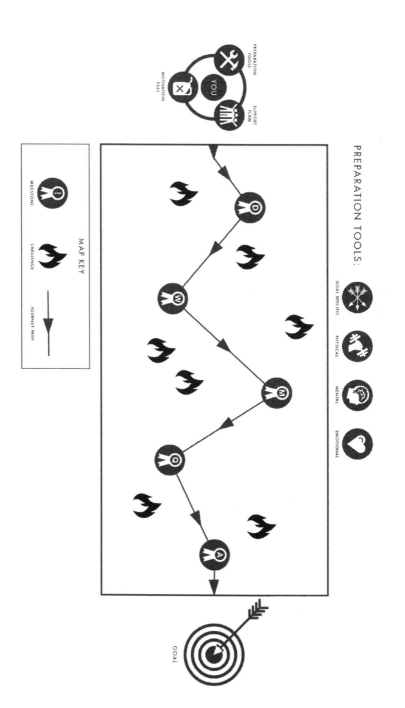

JOURNEY MAP:

PREPARATION TOOLS:

PREPARATION TOOLS

MOTIVATION FUEL

YOU

SUPPORT TEAM

GOAL SPECIFIC

PHYSICAL

MENTAL

EMOTIONAL

MAP KEY

MILESTONE

CHALLENGE

JOURNEY PATH

GOAL

Chapter 1

● ● ●

THE CEO'S JOURNEY

The "journey" is a metaphor for life—whether it's a road race or a life-long career. One of the lessons I learned from my race is the importance of reflecting on the journey. I encourage clients in my consulting business to ask themselves: "Where was I today, and where do I want to go tomorrow?" It's important for me to share with clients new ideas that encourage them to think more deeply. I also want to make sure they're consistently reflecting on where their journey is taking them.

It's not that people don't already think about these things, but people who spend a longer amount of time reflecting can get more out of their journeys than those who think less about where they are headed. There's a correlation between reflection, and the success you will achieve on your journey. Reflection allows people to stay focused on their values, what they are most passionate about, and how the individual steps they take align with their larger goals.

When the goals and direction of the journey are not clear, we must ask ourselves, "Where do I want the journey to take me? When people stop asking these questions, they wander off-course and get into trouble. We can be passionate about many things, not all of which are aligned toward achieving our goals, and this can cause us to wander. I challenge my clients to reflect on whether the choices they are making, and the path on which they are traveling, will help guide them in a positive direction during their journey.

SHAPING YOUR JOURNEY

An outstanding example of an Endurance Executive, Kim Nelson's journey has taken her farther than she ever thought possible. Kim is in her mid-40s and lives with her family outside of Toronto, Canada. Kim has served as CEO of two successful family-owned companies since 2011, with revenues totaling over $125 million, and has successfully completed 16 Ironman triathlons since 1998.

The ironman's format includes a 2.4-mile swim, followed by a 112-mile bike ride, and if that wasn't enough, a 26.2-mile run to finish. It's easy to feel in awe of how she can manage a busy schedule while performing at such a high level athletically.

When asked about how she's achieved the success she has today, Kim is quick to note that she wasn't always so confident in her abilities. In college, she did well as both a student and competitive swimmer. After graduating, she joined the family business, starting at the bottom and worked her way up.

Kim pinpoints her first ironman in 1998 as having given her the confidence to follow in her father's footsteps and fill the role of CEO when she took over the business in 2011. The ironman proved to be the first time she was able to consolidate her mental and physical skills and strength to reach a peak level of preparation and performance. She learned how a methodical training, planning, and preparation process, coupled with focus, perseverance, and discipline, could yield results she never thought possible.

Thanks to focus and discipline, over the years and through the races, Kim has steadily improved her time in 13 consecutive Ironman competitions. As both an athlete and businessperson, Kim has spent time reflecting on her values, her passions, and how she wants her journey to unfold. As a result, her path has taken her in an amazing direction.

WHAT MAKES US PASSIONATE?

After selling my company in 2009, I remained an employee, working under the people who bought the company. When different people asked me about selling the business, I explained that it was "the happiest and the saddest day of my life." I was happy because I had reached a milestone, but sad because a part of my identity went with the company.

Around that time, I had a chance meeting with author, motivational speaker, and thought leader, Simon Sinek. The timing of the meeting and the questions he asked me during our conversation helped me reflect on topics in a way I had not been able to do previously. In his writings, Sinek addresses the concept of starting with the "why." I asked myself "why" I sold my business. Simon helped me ask the right questions about what awaited me in the future.

This made me think about what makes me passionate, why I get out of bed, and why I do what I do. Endurance Executives frequently ask themselves, "Why?" and use their answers to help map out their personal journeys. A common thread running throughout the lives of successful CEOs is that they view those answers in the context of their personal, family, and business lives. They do not compartmentalize the *why* choices they make in their private lives as all that different from the *why* choices they make at work.

To fulfill the journey, everyone must understand that individual goals and choices matter in every context, whether at work or at home, when it comes to making the right decisions about how to prioritize. I've noticed that each successful CEO has their own "equation" when it comes to how they approach the personal, family, and business areas of their lives. They spend time thinking about how much of their lives are devoted to each component. Not everybody has a family, is married, or wants business to be the main part of the equation. Each person needs to figure out what equation is right for them.

PREPARATION FOR THE JOURNEY

When I set out to run the marathon, I was under the impression that, by following a 15-week program with a running group, and watching what I ate so I could lose weight, I did more than sufficient preparation. In spite of all of that, I still hit the wall at mile 14, and this is what inspired me to look closer at the notion of preparation.

As we define or redefine where we want our journeys to take us, we must contemplate what role preparation will play in getting us there. Preparation is a process that involves readying oneself for challenges, physically, emotionally, and mentally. Specific goals will require highly individualized preparation as well.

I do not want my readers to think that preparation is only needed for running a marathon. From a *Physical Preparation* standpoint, the more ambitious you are in your career, as with athletics, the more you need to take care of yourself. In a later chapter dedicated to physical preparation, we'll talk about self-care, a topic that sometimes gets over-looked. Self-care includes activities such as rest and laughter. These be-haviors have made a huge difference in my life, the lives of my clients, and people I've interviewed for this book.

The idea of *Emotional Preparation* carries different meanings for different people. In the journey through life, it can become easy to neglect our emotional side, and not adequately nurture our mental health. Over the last 20 years, everything I've learned surrounding emotional intelligence, success, and the endurance mindset revolves around self-awareness and self-regulation. More self-regulation would have helped me start the Marine Corps Marathon at a slower pace instead of letting the euphoria of running in such an electric environment (50,000 strong) get my adrenaline pumping to go out too fast.

Mental Preparation and *Emotional Preparation* need to be practiced day-after-day, and week-after-week, consistently, for years. The more ambitious people are, the more they need to consider making emotional preparation—especially self-care, rest, and recovery—a fundamental part of daily life. While people can throw themselves totally into their work, with no regard for mental wellness, and still become successful on a short-term basis, long-term success is driven by consistent mental preparation.

The last area of preparation is *Goal-specific Preparation,* and I credit one of my mentors, Verne Harnish, for showing me the value this particular type of preparation. He runs an international strategic planning and coaching consultancy. He talks about keeping your team smart, an idea that resonates deeply with me, because I am naturally curious with a thirst for knowledge. Harnish stresses that ongoing learning and development of your team's skill set is an absolute must when pursuing long-term goals.

In order to have consistent success, on an annual basis, over a long period of time, you must always learn more and more to keep up with changing trends, and the shifting needs of a developing company. In this way, you stay prepared for tackling the challenges that come along with strategic goal-setting. People who only invest in random learning from time-to-time do not see continuous upward growth in their work and personal lives. They peak quickly and can struggle to sustain momentum. People who avoid lifetime learning opportunities often rely heavily on their natural talents and abilities, but unfortunately, there is a limit to how far talent can take an individual without added knowledge to back them up.

THE PITFALLS

Along the journey, people face pitfalls such as:

*   Overwhelming stress
*   A desire to avoid discomfort rather than facing and working through difficult situations
*   Poor relationship management
*   Having no accountability.

Poor work+life balance manifests itself in the form of these symptoms, which are the most obvious signs that people are on their way to a career plateau, or have hit the wall. For ambitious executives trying to climb the ladder, these four areas are where we see them stumble most frequently.

STRESS

People believe they tolerate stress well when, in fact, it slowly runs your battery down before you realize it. In the last five years, I have been amazed by how people have learned to survive while being exposed to higher and higher levels of stress. In spite of all the data available to the public about the importance of stress management, people don't do enough on this front to care for themselves. The more ambitious you are, the more you need to invest time and energy into managing stress. The endurance mindset requires being aware of the influence stress has on your personal life, your family, and your professional existence.

AVOIDING DISCOMFORT

The need to avoid discomfort is natural to all human beings. When you have attained a certain level of success, this tendency can work against you. Pushing oneself to grow into the next level of performance always has periods of discomfort and growing pains. Many people self-sabotage because, fearing discomfort, they don't take enough risks, or they lack the mental fortitude to make it through the prolonged period of discomfort. The Endurance Executive looks at these uncomfortable times as necessary learning experiences. He or she takes the risks necessary to achieve ongoing growth, even when that means fighting through a tough or painful obstacle during the journey.

RELATIONSHIPS

Maintaining positive relationships in our lives is a key aspect of building and sustaining the endurance mindset. Many ambitious CEOs are willing to sacrifice in this area because they believe they do not have time for work, family, and friends. Their lives become all about work, which leads to difficulty forming meaningful relationships, loneliness, and isolation. Successful people pay attention and invest the appropriate amount of time to nurture meaningful connections with others.

With her demanding responsibilities, and insatiable drive to achieve, no one understands pitfalls and challenges quite as well as Kim Nelson. Kim mentioned the importance of managing stress when I asked her about some of the pitfalls faced by successful CEOs in their journeys... She relies greatly on training for races to help her deal with stress.

Over the years, training for Ironman's can leave your body in a perpetual state of discomfort and that has been helpful in business. Business people tend to make decisions that end the discomfort and uncertainty they are feeling, in many cases at their own expense. If you can tolerate discomfort associated with risk or uncertainty for a longer period of time, you can see a situation through a lot longer, gather more information and, ideally, make a more informed decision. Both of Kim's companies are based in Canada and have dealt with external economic challenges like currency fluctuation, and the complications that come along with working in the maturing corrugated cardboard industry. Kim and her team focus on the business basics and know they have to persevere, as the difficulties will improve over time.

Kim does an excellent job of relying on the people around her to hold her (and each other) accountable, and to provide much-needed advice in making complicated choices. Kim sees great value in surrounding oneself with others who can hold her accountable for her business decisions. When times get tough, CEOs can isolate themselves or stick with only a small, limited professional and social circle for support, but Nelson has done a good job of branching out and relying on other key business relationships to provide her with new insights.

I was curious about her experiences hitting the wall. How might someone so accomplished still "hit the wall?" Unfortunately, it happens to even the strongest, most talented and successful individuals. Nelson has a routine on the ready when she finds herself approaching the wall. Her body gives her warning signs, such as an overall feeling of negativity about her situation and a metallic taste in her mouth. The first important step for her is recognizing these signs, which indicate she is approaching a critical point.

Many people continue to push forward or don't recognize the urgency of their situations, so it is important for you to recognize you are in that zone. Kim's initial response is to engage in reassuring thoughts such as, "This will pass." Nelson also tries to refuel physically as soon as possible when she becomes aware that her energy stores are depleted and she needs fluids or solids. Once she has nourished herself physically, she tries to expand her focus to more self-aware, positive thoughts that involve trusting her body and the time spent training.

The last thing Kim does to help her avoid hitting the wall is to look at her watch and project when the discomfort will pass. Generally, she gives herself an hour, but has found that the worst part of the experience passes in 20 to 30 minutes. In a nine- to 12-hour race, 20 minutes can seem like an eternity, but this process helped her through each difficult moment when Kim hit the wall during an Ironman race.

THE ACCOUNTABILITY LOOP

The last potential pitfall, the accountability loop, can be particularly challenging for many CEOs, because certain high-level executives possess too much autonomy. As a result, they lack the system of checks and balances that tends to hold lower-tier workers accountable. Total autonomy in the absence of accountability creates a dangerous dynamic.

In the days after the marathon, I thought about the impact that stress had on my preparation. I thought about the amount of training I put myself through and the feedback I got from my family. I wondered if maybe I hadn't found the right balance yet. I probably handled the relationship element of the equation well, but in terms of accountability, I needed a better coach.

As the weeks passed and I had more time to reflect on my experiences, I realized that I wanted to become more adept at working with all of my clients on subjects that relate to passion, desire, and commitment. I also wanted to get my own life and thoughts organized around my goals, so that as I gave my clients goals, I was equally as rigorous. I wanted to lead by example. We instituted an improved follow-up plan with clients, so that after we reviewed their goals and saw progress, we would still be there to offer encouragement, feedback, and accountability.

After a month or two, I concluded the most important thing about revisiting the accountability loop was that, in order for me to grow my business, be a better husband and father, I needed to grow and improve my support team to focus on passion, desire, and commitment. In this way, I made sure that I would not succumb to the accountability loop pitfall. The next time I go on a marathon adventure, I will build a larger team, and ask them to hold me accountable in a different way from what I expected out of my last team.

Our goal in highlighting these four areas of focus is so that you can see pitfalls you've been susceptible to in the past, and to increase awareness to hopefully prevent future stumbles. The landscape changes for everyone, all the time, and people who might not have endured or encountered certain difficulties in their pasts will do so eventually.

If you continue to grow, remain self-aware, prepared, and are held accountable by a strong support team, there's an outstanding chance you will overcome these hurdles.

CHAPTER 1 SUMMARY

The "journey" is a metaphor for life—whether it's a road race or a life-long career. One of the lessons I learned from my race is the importance of reflecting on the journey.

Shaping Your Journey means to reflect in order to set a direction and give yourself goals that will bring fulfillment. Kim Nelson, an outstanding example of an Endurance Executive, has gone farther on her journey than she ever thought possible, thanks to her frequent reflection on her direction in life and her ability to execute against her goals.

What Makes Us Passionate is a critical question Endurance Executives always ask themselves as they prepare to embark on a journey.

Preparation for the Journey: When I set out to run the marathon, I was under the impression that I had all the tools to be successful. What I realized was that my level of preparation was not nearly what it could have been. Even though I had seen this with many of my clients, I still committed the same mistake for my race.

The Pitfalls: Along the journey, people face pitfalls that will increase their chances of failure, such as:

* **Overwhelming Stress:** People often feel that they can manage stress, but as CEOs and other leaders become more ambitious it becomes difficult to manage competing priorities, and stress management can present as more of a challenges.

* **Avoiding Discomfort:** The need to avoid discomfort is natural to all human beings. When you have attained a certain level of success, this tendency can resurface and work against you. Many CEOs and other leaders aren't motivated to endure this type of feeling because they think they are past "it."

* **Relationships:** Maintaining positive relationships in our lives is key to building and sustaining the endurance mindset. It gets

very lonely as a CEO and/or leader; it is important to have strong relationships to avoid this pitfall.

* **The Accountability Loop:** The last potential pitfall, the accountability loop, can be particularly challenging for many CEOs, because certain high-level executives possess too much autonomy and have no one to hold them accountable.

REFLECTIONS:

Everyone hits a wall at some point and everyone faces one of more of these challenges in some way, shape, or form.

1. What potential challenges do you see on the horizon?
2. Which of the four pitfalls do you struggle with?

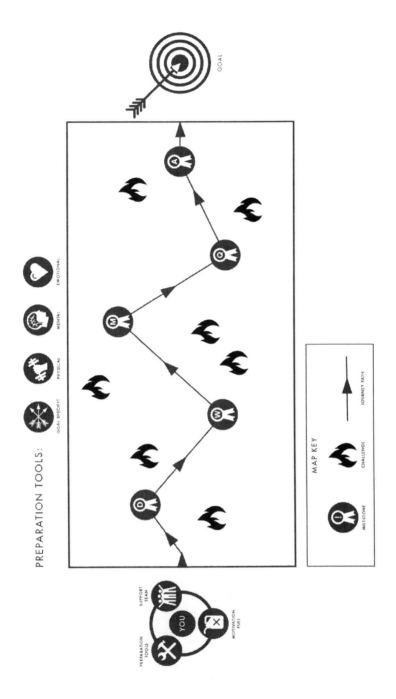

JOURNEY MAP:

Chapter 2

• • •

MOTIVATIONAL FUEL FOR THE JOURNEY

Marathons are symbolic, so a lot of runners dedicate their race to some-one. It's safe to say that, if not for an outstanding source of inspiration, there's a good chance runners wouldn't do marathons in the first place. People dedicate themselves to a cause or passion, and that higher purpose serves as fuel to take on such an endeavor.

During mile 15 of my race, my body ached to the point that my survival instinct screamed, "Step-over-step, five seconds, ten seconds, one minute, two minutes, get to the next mile, stretch, stretch, continue." I thought about the things that were most important to me, and what I was passionate about. Given the extreme pain, the thought of having to go more than 11 more miles was daunting, to say the least. That's where passion, desire, and commitment started coming through in my thoughts and actions.

I also focused my mind on the ideas I'd considered during recent moments of reflection, and took strength from those thoughts. Passion can lead to feelings of gratefulness. Passion can manifest itself in the form of love, or the pursuit of a goal. Contemplating your passions can get you into the right mindset for success—no small feat for a person who has hit the wall.

In my experience, whether I'm pursuing personal goals, leading the company I used to own, or coaching CEOs at my current job, success is dependent upon the way we individually relate to and experience passion, desire, and commitment. As I've worked with people over the last four years at the C-level and VP-level, more often than not, one of these elements is missing, contributing to the challenges executives face while trying to get to the next level of performance.

In your journey, you will come across individuals—friendly travelers—who are memorable because they build their lives around certain valuable principles and behaviors that inspire others. A person who stands out in my mind as representing desire, passion, and commitment is Brian Hightower.

MEET BRIAN

If you follow rugby on NBC Universal, you will see Brian commentating on the matches. We were fraternity brothers at the College of William & Mary. He had come to W&M to play wide receiver for the football team, but decided not to continue playing due to the academic rigors of the school. Instead, taking advantage of his unique combination of speed, strength, and a low center of gravity, he took up rugby and went on to set a number of records. Many people pointed out what a natural he was at rugby. Brian always put on a good show, whether he was scoring or tackling someone to get the ball.

College came and went, and Brian headed west to Aspen to see what adventures might be there for him. He continued to focus on rugby and set a goal to make the US World Cup Team. It took him about five years, but not only did he make the US World Cup Sevens team, he went on to captain the side. When I was planning to write this book, I thought Brian's insight, from competing at a world class level in rugby to endurance racing, could be an interesting addition. As an athlete, he was able to understand the propensity to hit the wall during preparation for, or participation in, a match or endurance event.

A great deal of preparation and hard work went into Brian being able to play his sport at the highest level. I asked him to talk to me about hitting the wall in that setting. Like many other elite athletes, Hightower credits his success to the amount of physical preparation he put in, which allowed him to ascend to playing at the World Cup. Many times he hit the wall in practice, given the level of conditioning players are put through to prepare for that legendary match. His belief that "the pain will end at some point" assisted him through these dark moments. He recounted how his teammates, overcome by exhaustion, dropped out of drills one by one, while Hightower continued to be one of the last men standing almost every time.

Even as his body reached a point where it did not want to go on, Brian understood the finite nature of pain. It would be hard to dismiss the anecdotes provided by an athlete at this level. Since Rugby in the United States is not a primetime sport where players are paid salaries, all US players hold down day jobs, and they put their time in purely for the love of the game. For the passion!

PASSION IS BROAD; DESIRE IS SPECIFIC

Whereas passion is more of a broad positive feeling, something that creates a lot of energy and enthusiasm, desire is more acute and specific. I'm passionate about wine. I might not always *desire* wine, but I'm passionate about wine. I might desire a glass of great champagne to celebrate the conclusion of this book, but that's different from wanting to have a glass every night. Passion is more broadly stated, while desire is more specific to a moment or particular goal.

It's easy for people to be passionate about an industry or a topic, and use that as a source of energy for expressing their desire. Desire is about the details, the method and approach. If you want to have continued growth throughout your career, you must be specific about what you want to accomplish. You must recruit desire to compliment and expand upon your passion. Sometimes, this means making a plan, or a "contract" of sorts, with yourself. A contract is the ultimate marriage of passion and desire with commitment.

Brian Hightower also talked about his desire to be the best, and creating a contract with himself was one of the keys to his success. If you have an ambitious goal, the desire to be the best will push you to the edge in pursuing your biggest goals. While you don't want to get injured, you have to explore the edge to make sure you get the most out of your performance. The edge can illicit fear of pain, or fear of hitting the wall. At that point, Brian suggests asking, "What contract do I have with myself?"

Hightower's contract concept explores the willingness to make sacrifices in the pursuit of a larger goal. Hightower's desire to be the best aligns directly with the notion of commitment. While Hightower didn't initially acknowledge the factor of self-questioning, his passion for rugby is directly tied to his desire for success. This manifests in his need to make a contract. One of these elements, by itself, is not enough to reach an ambitious goal and stay there. The combination of the three give an endurance executive the motivation to be successful over a long period of time.

As with Brian's contract, the practices people engage in, in order to achieve commitment, become extremely important to the success of the journey. If people do not set high standards of achievement, they may self-sabotage by never pushing themselves to explore the edge, or to fully self-actualize. Behaviors such as inaction, procrastination, or not actively working toward your goals by completing small necessary tasks, encourage failure. They limit your potential. You must have enough commitment to overcome self-limiting beliefs. What is the use of having great potential if you never push yourself to fully reach that potential?

The moment people stop trying to achieve—whether it's during a race, or in the midst of building a career—is when there's a breakdown in commitment. In my racing experience, I knew when I hit the wall that I had to endure and conserve my energy. Conserving my energy played an important part in preventing self-limitation and self-sabotage.

PASSION, DESIRE, AND COMMITMENT: THE ENDURANCE EXECUTIVE'S MOTIVATIONAL FUEL

If you're going to attempt to develop the three parts of an Endurance Executive's motivational fuel, it's important that you feel clear on what each of them means to you. Start with passion, and ask yourself how much it burns within you, then make a game plan around desire. Then build a contract with yourself, which will ensure your personal commitment to the goal. While I am passionate about fitness and running, what kept me going when I hit the wall was my desire to finish the race and not to walk any more than I had to. I committed to endure a lot of pain, to stay focused and to not give up.

Commitment is a holistic process that engages mind, body, and spirit. Commitment includes how you perform at work, as well as in your personal life. Some executives can have strong commitment in their jobs, but struggle with physical health or personal relationships. Commitment is a lifestyle, and compartmentalization becomes nearly impossible when one is living that committed lifestyle.

The Endurance Executive thinks, "I need to be consistent, to critically examine my home life as much as my work life." When one part of your life becomes successful at the expense of another, the aspect you sacrifice drags down your overall prosperity, making you less successful when it comes to the big picture.

When the Endurance Executive reflects upon his or her passions, has a desire, and makes a commitment, there can be a conflict of interest—a point where the individual feels they must make sacrifices in one area of their lives in order to fulfill their commitment to another. For example, imagine a busy upwardly mobile entrepreneur taking account of his daily priorities, responsibilities and commitments. He may feel that, due to his busy schedule, he does not have time for personal care and recovery, and opts to sacrifice time spent on physical activity and meal planning in order to spend more time at work. Unfortunately, this way of thinking will catch up to him eventually and result in poor physical health. It's hard to run a thriving business while dealing with the fallout of heart disease or diabetes.

We all need to make choices. If you are considering sacrificing one aspect of your life's commitments for another, and doing so in isolation without asking for guidance from others, you probably won't get a well-rounded view of the potential consequences of that sacrifice. When evaluating your commitments, discuss your feelings with people who are close to you, including your support team, your spouse, or best friend, because these people can give you feedback on your performance in multiple areas of your life, and help guide you in making the best choices.

Often, when we make decisions on sacrifices in isolation, we carry out biased, subjective dialogues inside our own minds, rather than seeking the guidance of those who are able to view our commitments from a more objective perspective. We should be having discussions about commitment, and the sacrifices that can come along with commitment, with people we trust and love.

WORK+LIFE

This is where we explore the ways in which we can organize our thoughts and behaviors to facilitate healthy connection between the different aspects of our lives. Sometimes people use the term "balance," but a more appropriate term is "interplay."

"Balance" is flawed, because it is impossible to balance two elements that are not of equal value. When you look at life versus work, the amount of time you spend working is oftentimes greater than the amount of time you spend taking care of responsibilities outside of work, including personal and recovery time. If we consider the number of hours we spend devoted to each element of our lives, from family and personal, to work time, we will generally see that most of us prioritize one above the others. This makes total balance very difficult, so you must critically evaluate the interplay between these conflicting commitments.

Ask yourself these important questions:

* How committed are you to your goals?
* How committed are you to self-improvement?
* How committed are you to your family, your wife, and your children?

PASSION VERSUS DESIRE

Most technology CEOs were intensely passionate about technology when they started their careers. They had a great idea, pursued it, and their business grew. The demands of performing well in a mid-size company are much different than those of performing well as a CEO for a small business. As your company becomes larger, taking on the role of executive VP or a C-level at an enterprise-level business becomes even greater than it was for the mid-size company. Our aforementioned technology CEO's passion may still be there, but what might have changed is the desire to remain a CEO, considering the ever-increasing amount of work needed. Do they feel the same way about IT? The more removed they become from the original reason they started their business (such as, designing effective software), the more disconnected they feel from their passion.

If a clear goal cannot be easily visualized, that desire fades away. The idea of success in their day-to-day work life is no longer about creating effective software; it's now about leading teams, budgeting, and overseeing tedious operations. The CEO might still feel passionately about software, but his or her desire shifts its focus and momentum can be lost.

DESIRE VERSUS COMMITMENT

Desire and commitment, as tools in the Endurance Executive's toolkit, get confused as well. My beautiful daughter is 14 years old, and she has a specific desire to go to college in New York City, possibly Columbia or NYU. I'm convinced that she has desire at 14, but does she have the commitment to do whatever it takes?

Will she do the work, get the right grades, and succeed on the SAT test? Will she do enough extracurricular activities to make her a desirable candidate for those schools? I'm not sure. What makes a goal challenging is a higher likelihood of failure. People say they're committed to certain goals, and convince themselves that they are, but their behaviors often indicate that they are not committed. In this situation, they are confusing desire and commitment.

I've experience this misguided attitude with great frequency in my line of work. When a person who is confusing desire with commitment tells me they are committed, I point out specific behaviors in order to challenge their beliefs. People who are truly committed show behaviors that support their devotion to a goal or journey.

In his book, *Blink*, Malcolm Gladwell asserts that people who have worked in management, leadership, or other specialty positions are perceptive in evaluating people's behavior patterns. They also see the same behaviors repeated over and over by many different workers and job candidates, in many different situations. Recognizing behavior patterns enables them to identify when there is a disconnect between what people are saying and how they are behaving.

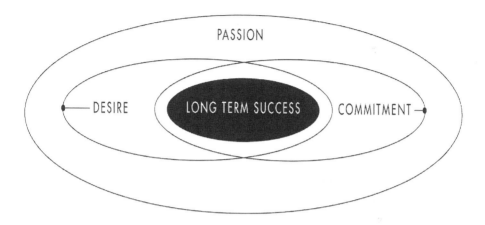

COMMITMENT IS AN ENDURANCE SPORT

If you are all alone when you hit the wall, making it through is about composure, and choosing to relax rather than panic. After a person hits that metaphorical wall, then finds a way to stabilize and begin working on making changes, it's important to think about passion, commitment, and desire—because these three ideas become the fuel for making it to the finish line. They are the foundation of the Endurance Mindset. You will never achieve an endurance mindset if you don't have a clear idea regarding what you're passionate about. You must also know what your short-, medium- and long- term desires are and what kind of commitment you are willing to put forth toward all three.

A passionate educator might think, "Well, I'm passionate about teaching. I have the desire to be a college professor, so I will need a PhD." At that point, motivated by a passion for teaching, the possibility of attaining a PhD becomes tangible, though it might not be easy. The individual would need to go back to school, and set aside time to put forth a thesis. Their passion will not dictate their success—only open up the possibility. Their desire will go a long way toward getting them back in school, but only true commitment will ultimately result in a professorship.

Remember Brian from earlier in the chapter? He has a great example of passion, desire, and commitment. In addition to playing rugby out west, Hightower started getting into different types of endurance races. A fledgling team endurance race caught his eye: the Eco Challenge. This race was a 24-hour, 300-mile team event, including two men and two women per team. Disciplines covered included a range of grueling activities on the racecourse: trekking, mountaineering, whitewater canoeing, etc. The first Eco Challenge was held in Utah in 1995, and since he was in such great condition after competing in the US World Cup Rugby team, Hightower went on to compete in the 2000 race in Borneo.

Our discussion focused on hitting the wall at the Eco Challenge, and Hightower recalled a part of the race that happened on a beach. He had just concluded a particularly long swim in open water, midway through the event, when the pain hit in his stomach. At the end of the swim, he reported being cramped up, and lying on the beach. Luckily, his team helped him get through this moment, just as he had done for others during different parts of the race. Success came from a combination of their encouragement and his belief that failure was not an option. Little by little, Hightower was able to get up from the beach and resume the race.

"I didn't panic like many people do when they hit the wall in this race setting. I wasn't going to let my team down. I just needed to gather myself before continuing. The combination of their support and my personal contract to the team, regarding finishing the race and failure not being an option, helped me get through his painful stage of the race."

In the next chapter we're going to put concepts and goals on paper in order to get a better understanding of our own passions, desires, and commitments. If we don't think about working through our conflicts in an organized fashion, we stay in career plateaus. This is why certain CEOs see their own business stalling, or failing. They don't get organized enough around the three key elements, which are the building blocks of success.

When you're not getting this right, it's hard to move forward. For the Endurance Executive, motivation is fuel, and you will run out of fuel if you don't have a clear understanding of passion, desire, and commitment.

CHAPTER 2 SUMMARY

Marathons are symbolic, so a lot of runners dedicate their race to someone. It's safe to say that, if not for an outstanding source of inspiration, there's a good chance runners wouldn't do marathons in the first place. When people dedicate themselves to a cause or passion that higher purpose serves as fuel to take them on such an endeavor.

PASSION IS BROAD; DESIRE IS SPECIFIC

Whereas passion is more of a broad, positive feeling—something that creates a lot of energy and enthusiasm—desire is a more specific, tangible thing that someone wants to get and/or accomplish.

PASSION, DESIRE, AND COMMITMENT: THE ENDURANCE EXECUTIVE'S MOTIVATIONAL FUEL

If you're going to attempt to develop the three parts of an Endurance Executive's motivational fuel, it's important that you feel clear on what each of them means to you. Start with passion: What you are passionate about? Then think about what your specific desire is in an area that you are passionate about. Finally, build a contract with yourself, which will ensure your personal commitment to fulfill your goal.

WORK+LIFE

This is new way to look at "balance" so that work and life aren't pitted against each other. The Endurance Executive chooses how much to allocate to work and how much to allocate to life so they can accomplish their goals.

PASSION VERSUS DESIRE

These two items are often mistaken as one in the same, but they are not. An Endurance Executive invests time reflecting on each to help differentiate between the two.

DESIRE VERSUS COMMITMENT

Desire and commitment, as tools in the Endurance Executive's toolkit, get confused as well. Desire is a specific goal, while commitment is what you are willing to do to reach that goal.

COMMITMENT IS AN ENDURANCE SPORT

If you are all alone when you hit the wall, making it through is about composure. An Endurance Executive chooses to relax rather than panic. In order to persevere through this difficult moment, you have to use your motivational fuel—passion, commitment, and desire—to make it to the finish line.

REFLECTIONS:

There are a few ways to think about these lessons in the context of a simple question.

1. If you look at your life during the last five years, what have you been the most passionate about?
2. Can you segment that into the individual aspects of personal, family and work elements?

For example, you might say, "I'm passionate about my children's sports success. My desire is to watch them play all their games." The commitment is thinking about what you'll have to do in order to make sure that happens. So, does the commitment entail not taking meetings after 5 p.m.? Is it not taking any meetings after 4 p.m. on Fridays? What limits will you place on your life in order to fulfill your commitment in that one area?

A look back over our lives, our work, and what we've learned can be a great endurance building exercise. Ask yourself, "What did I do the last time I hit the wall—experienced the death of a loved one, was dumped by a significant other, got a bad grade, or lost a big-money business deal?" We can all learn a great deal when we reflect that far back. Just writing this book has encouraged me to reflect on 25 years of my life, and it's been a gift.

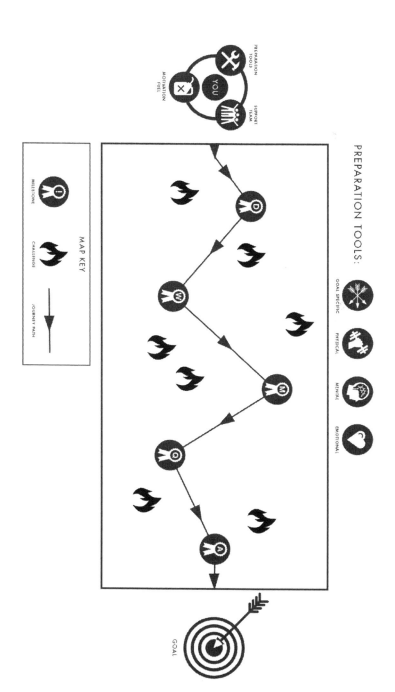

PREPARATION TOOLS:

JOURNEY MAP.

MILESTONE

CHALLENGE

JOURNEY PATH

MAP KEY

PREPARATION TOOLS

MOTIVATION FUEL

YOU

SUPPORT TEAM

GOAL SPECIFIC

PHYSICAL

MENTAL

EMOTIONAL

GOAL

Chapter 3

IDENTIFY YOUR GOALS

Some of the biggest challenges faced by successful leaders in their 20s, or high-level leaders in their 30s and 40s, is setting an appropriate and achievable number of goals. Ambition is a wonderful thing, but if you're setting a lot of goals, you can experience "goal clutter." When you have too many goals, it's easy to lose sight of the most important ones, causing your foundation to weaken so that challenges escalate to serious problems.

The first step to take in avoiding goal clutter is to establish a positive relationship between your level of ambition and your fear of failure. A lot of people think it's good to be driven by the fear of failure. Instead, it's preferable to be driven 80 to 90 percent by ambition, and 10 to 20 percent by fear of failure. When balanced in a healthy relationship, ambition and fear both challenge and complement one another. Having some fear of failure helps you avoid becoming over-confident.

Ideas about setting big goals have been around as popular concepts now for a couple of decades. In their 1996 book, *Built to Last*, noted business thought leaders Jim Collins and Jerry Porras coined the expression BHAG. BHAG stands for the "big, hairy, audacious goal" that encourages companies to get focused around one overarching goal. This continues to influence executives to set big goals, but when you go after these and fall short, it can prove disheartening.

In the face of failure, you can become driven by the fear, as opposed to staying focused on making the goal. Fear of failure is similar to adding salt to a dish when cooking: A small amount can help a dish taste better, but too much ruins the meal.

AMBITION VERSUS FEAR OF FAILURE: FINDING THE RIGHT BALANCE

CEOs and high-level executives can be their own worst enemies early in their careers. When they start to enjoy some measure of success, they often begin to push themselves even harder by setting many different types of goals. If someone sets seven goals and only meets three of them, that's four times that they plant a seed for the fear of failure. Consistent underperformance on goals can negatively influence self-confidence and how we perceive our skills and talents. It pushes us from one extreme, driven by pure ambition with no fear of failure, toward the other extreme of less ambition, lower confidence, and great fear of failure.

The healthy middle ground is 80/20, with the danger area at 50/50. Once we hit the 50/50 point, ambition plummets. Negative outcomes rapidly balloon into thought patterns influencing our self-esteem faster and more deeply than positive outcomes. If you experience a series of failures and develop negative inertia, the pendulum will swing toward the extreme, defined by a lack of ambition. In this case, you're motivated only by the fear of failure—a toxic, shortsighted source of motivation.

A good example of this is when athletes over-train. They don't want to experience failure, so they push beyond what their bodies can handle and injure themselves. In the white collar world, when there is a big presentation to the board or a major customer, leaders who fear failure or have too many goals can over-prepare. The stress surrounding that affects their sleep, interactions with people, and ultimately, their performance. As CEOs and high-level executives set goals, they must be mindful of that ratio between ambition and fear of failure.

"Ambitious" is a word often used to describe people in the workplace who are looking to climb the corporate ladder. To be ambitious carries the implication that you're trying to do something in a shorter amount of time than expected. Someone has an "ambitious plan" when they're trying to accomplish a lot. Ambition can be taught and used in the same way we use desire—to visualize a goal and become specific in our plans to achieve that goal.

When I have taken time to reflect, I've realized that, at times, I have reacted in an overly ambitious way. An example of this was my strategy for the Marine Corps Marathon. At the beginning, I had no fear of hitting the wall, so I went all out. Fear of failure might have caused me to start out slow and speed up once I found a good pace. The fear of failure, accompanied by the pain of hitting the wall, came a little too late, but it was enough to provide a healthy dose humility and reality.

Ambition is directly related to self-confidence. We can acknowledge that a little bit of fear inspires humility, which is good. However, when a higher ratio of fear controls your actions, this leads to uncertainty about your life and work, and a decline in self-confidence. Goal attainment, on the other hand, allows an Endurance Executive to nourish his or her sense of ambition and self-confidence.

DISTRACTIONS HAPPEN

Another major challenge when identifying, prioritizing, and pursuing goals is managing distractions. They are an inescapable part of daily life. I admire and study successful parents, spouses, CEOs, and sales leaders, and I'm interested in learning how they deal with distractions. Many have an uncanny ability to tune out that which could interrupt their daily progress toward completing tasks and achieving goals.

I have learned from these people that if we can proactively think about what distractions might come down the pike, we can be prepared to avoid them. People are not always realistic when factoring potential distractions into their planning. For example, I'm training for another marathon, yet my 20-year college reunion will happen three weeks before the race. I would be naïve to think that weekend won't be disruptive to my training schedule.

A very ambitious executive might be unrealistic in assuming that the pending birth of a child won't distract him or her from their important corporate plans. While we can't anticipate everything that might throw us off course, when we plan for potential interruptions, it helps us increase the probability of success. We are also allowed to develop countermeasures, or reprioritize as needed.

PACE OF WORK

In my work as an executive coach and strategic advisor, my clients and I talk about the pace of work and how it is important to find "quiet space." Quiet space can be defined as time alone, or with family, but not thinking about work. We also talk about rest, and how much downtime we are getting in conjunction with overall hours spent working. During all the years I traveled (200,000 miles per year), when I made an effort to track the number of days I spent on the road, it made a difference in my mental health, scheduling and general planning. In that way, I was able to make a conscious effort every year to be gone fewer days. Some people might track their miles, and plan for fewer, but that would not have helped me. Theoretically, I could travel less miles, but still be away from home and family just as much. I wanted to work toward what was best for my family, and that meant altering my pace of work.

We have to make sure the strategies we create to control our pace of work also align with our life and career goals. For endurance leaders and executives, as we get older, it becomes all about working smarter, not harder. That expression meant something different in my 30s than it does now in my 40s. In my 30's I traveled a great deal and didn't spend as much time at home as I would have liked to so I was very careful about how I would allocate time to non-family after hours events. In my 40's, I travel far less than in my 30's so I attend more of these types of events than before because I am around more and spend more time with my family. I'm sure it will change again when I hit my 50s. If we're going to work smarter, not harder, what should our goal equation look like?

These ideas, questions, and reflections helped me understand the importance of balancing and managing work+life responsibilities and goals. The work+life equation appeals to people who are pragmatic, task-oriented, and regimented. Only about 50 percent of the population fits that description. The other 50 percent, being more right-brained and non-linear in their worldviews, struggle with this. They think about the notion of balance as a nice ideal to aspire to, while more ambitious people see something literal and achievable in balancing work+life. It is a focus with which they can connect.

Many people become frustrated after years of seeking the "right way" to go about conducting their lives and balancing their careers. For those who've experienced this frustration, work+life is a concept that seems logical and makes sense. The "right way" can mean any number of things, depending upon one's circumstances, job, and individual needs. In the context of the Endurance Mindset, work+life has a way of helping one to determine the key factors that will contribute to goal achievement. This equation breaks down big, challenging issues into a formula that makes it easier for logic-minded people to assess the value of their daily responsibilities.

During my marathon, from miles 17 through 20, I thought about the work+life balance, working smarter instead of harder, and how to reconcile all this with setting the right number of attainable, yet challenging goals. The reflecting I did during those miles provided me with some clarity regarding elements of creating and managing goals. After the race, I thought about my mistakes, so I started writing my ideas down. I later used those recorded thoughts to help others with their personal and professional growth. Writing about one's thoughts and responses captures our realizations in a tangible form we can revisit. The wisdom we gain from this self-evaluation increases the chance for success in the future.

WISDOM FROM THE PROS

Cal Ripken was one of my favorite athletes when I was growing up in the DC area, and his record epitomizes endurance. He caught the attention of baseball fans with his impressive consecutive game playing streak. The previous record, set by a man named Lou Gehrig, had stood unbroken since 1939. The second closest player, Everett Scott, came in at 1307 straight games. Ripken broke the record on September 5, 1995 by playing 2,131 games, surpassing Gehrig's mark. Did he finally take a game off after this? Not Cal. Ripken's record spanned 2,632 games, over 16 seasons, and after three years, in 1998, he finally took a day off!

Ripken eventually retired in 2001. He parlayed his baseball success into business success by starting a company, Ripken Baseball, with his brother. They built youth stadiums and created training programs for young people. Cal also acquired several minor league baseball teams.

Ripken did a lot of writing after baseball. In 2007, he released three books, including *Get in the Game: 8 Elements of Perseverance That Make the Difference.* In this book, he outlines what he feels made a difference in his career and enabled him to break the consecutive games record. The two chapters I want to highlight, which reinforce topics we discuss in this book, are his chapters on preparation and life management.

Ripken's process for mental preparation was an impressive aspect of readying himself for a game. He credits some of his success to having a pre-game routine that kept him sharp, especially during the season in which he broke the consecutive games record. It was a media circus that season, but Ripken made it clear he would only talk to the media before the first game of every series. In order to keep his mental energy levels high, he did not want to get caught up in the hype, and lose focus from the more important aspects of each individual game. This routine helped give the media what they wanted, while Ripken kept his own head clear, and his game day priorities at the forefront of his mind.

Ripken downplayed the goal of breaking the record, but he did a great job of breaking down the key things that needed to happen for him to break the record. Setting rules around media and being proactive supported his pursuit of the goal.

For Endurance Executives, mental energy is a source of focus, inspiration and recovery. By planning around goals, the Endurance Executive does not allow outside hype or distractions to interfere with his or her performance.

Ripken has an insightful chapter on life management. He had a very clear work + life equation. He addresses the fact that if you strictly separate your personal from your professional goals, you are bound to ask yourself which is more important. Ripken didn't like the perspective of prioritizing one over the other, as both are very important. While working as a professional baseball player, he went to great lengths to see his children on his days off. His organization supported that choice. He appreciated the Orioles' support in providing options for players to spend time with family, and it was a contributing factor in why he never considered playing anywhere else.

What stood out in Ripken's physical preparation was not how hard or how much he worked compared to the other guys, but that he learned as he got older to take care of himself. He chose to modify his workout routine to correlate with what his body told him it needed for recovery and health. Baseball players are not always the fittest people, as many in the sport are overweight.

Ripken also addresses how mental energy and wellness plays a key role in physical fitness. He didn't understand this mind-body connection clearly until after he stopped playing, and gained 15 pounds in his first year off the field. Along with the weight gain, his mental energy dropped compared to past years. For Ripken, like many other successful athletes and endurance executives, successful performance was not just about training the body, but also the mind.

In his book, Ripken points out that the company you work for plays a huge role in the pursuit of a balanced work+life equation. Does your company support your work + life equation?

SETTING GOALS

When setting a goal, ask yourself why it is important:

* Why does it matter?
* What has kept you from committing to putting goals on paper?
* How will personal, family, and professional goals compete with one another?

When we go deeper in our commitment and put goals on paper, we see patterns emerging in our ways of thinking and behaving. In my experience doing goal exercises with CEOs and other senior-level executives, I see patterns in what people struggle with, whether it's personal, family, or professional aspects of their lives.

Successful people are passionate about personal pursuits and about their families. Often, they haven't given enough thought to the amount of time and energy that will be required for the personal or family goals, given the demanding professional goals they set. Business goals are always the easiest for a CEO or high-level leaders to put on paper because they have to do this regularly. Many executives are more familiar with writing about their business needs than addressing their family and personal needs.

The act of putting any goal on paper is a catalyst moment, when a goal shifts from abstraction to a literal translation that enables one to see and explicitly commit to the goal. CEOs and senior leaders have a bias of not wanting to fall short on the commitments they make, which can cause them to hesitate to put a goal on paper. An Endurance Executive puts all goals on paper, to establish whether or not he or she has the energy and time to successfully attain them.

As you start looking at different goals, time becomes a key factor. Imagine the time that you have as a pie. How it will be sliced is dependent upon how much value you place on each of your goals. Are you going to invest 10 percent of your time on personal, 30 percent on family, and 60 percent at work? Defining and breaking down time encourages people to think about personal and family needs.

It might be difficult for you to commit to your personal goal if you're only allocating only 1 percent of your time toward that focus. That would be a low priority commitment. You can either have goals with low priority percentages, or you can calibrate, moderate, and say, "I'm going to commit 50 percent work, 30 percent family, and 20 percent personal." If these percentages are representative of time, we just need to align our goals relative to the time (in hours) spent on each.

People have the desire to achieve well-rounded and fair percentages for all three. However, when individuals make decisions about how they will split their time without consulting others, they can make poor choices. In order to increase the chances of your success with goal prioritization, after you do your first pass of identifying your goals, engage with those around you. Ask friends, family members, and colleagues to give you feedback.

In the next chapter, we'll discuss how you can have an ongoing dialogue with those who have your best interests at heart—people who can give you feedback to help you make great decisions that align with your goals. They will also hold you accountable for sticking to your commitments.

CONSERVATION VERSUS CONSUMPTION

At the end of this chapter, you'll find my goal matrix tool. With this tool, you will be able to see what the Endurance Equation looks like on paper. If we don't map the equation in the most literal sense, we won't think about a notion I refer to as "conservation versus consumption."

Most people rely too much on consumption, due to a fundamental belief in an abundance of resources. I'm a big believer in trusting in abundance. An abundant mindset says, "I have plenty of time, energy, experience, and I've been extremely successful." All these thoughts help leaders, especially successful CEOs, but abundance comes and goes based on factors that are not always within your control. Economic changes, for example, can lead to abundance one year, and struggles the next.

When people stumble, they think they don't have choices. They *do* have choices. The first important choice they need to make is between conservation and consumption. A conservation mindset states, "I need to conserve so I can take care of personal, family, and professional needs." Conservation mindsets acknowledge life's feasts, as well as the possibility of famine.

TRAINING FOR THE RIGHT RACE

In life and other long distance endurance events, success is about making the right sacrifices. If you feel you're always sacrificing, with little gain, then maybe it's not the right race for you. The best way to make sure that you're training for the right race is to use what you've learned in this chapter to map out your goals and address them from a perspective of conservation, not consumption.

In a metaphorical way, we can train for life's marathons, but it's really a triathlon we're seeking to complete. The three aspects of family, personal, and work life form a triad of needs. When I was training for the marathon, I realized I needed to prepare for all three in my endurance equation. I committed to my family that if I did this again in the future I would approach it like a triathlon, making sure I spent as much time as possible with them, rather than letting the training own me.

	BUSINESS	FAMILY	PERSONAL	
DAILY				
WEEKLY				
MONTHLY				
QUARTERLY				
ANNUAL				

People
Stretch
Solutions

GOALS — HOW TO ORGANIZE

CHAPTER 3 SUMMARY

One of the greatest challenges faced by successful leaders in their 20s—
or high-level leaders in their 30s and 40s—is setting an appropriate and
achievable number of goals. Frequently, leaders find that they have far
too many goals and need to reassess their priorities. In

AMBITION VERSUS FEAR OF FAILURE: FINDING THE RIGHT BALANCE

CEOs and high-level executives can be their own worst enemies early in
their careers. When they start to enjoy some measure of success, they often
begin to push themselves even harder by setting many different types of
goals. At this point, they must be careful of failing to reach multiple goals,
because the fear of failure starts to perpetuate with each failure.

DISTRACTIONS HAPPEN

Another major challenge encountered when identifying, prioritizing,
and pursuing goals is how to manage distractions. They are an inescapable part of daily life.

PACE OF WORK

In my work as an executive coach and strategic advisor, my clients and
I talk about the pace of work and how it is important to find "quiet
space." As CEOs and leaders grow more successful they have to pay
more attention to the amount of work they do to maintain a level of
quality and success in attaining their goals.

SETTING GOALS

This is the first step in showing a heightened level of commitment when we put goals on paper. We see patterns emerging in our ways of thinking and behaving the moment it leaves our head and becomes visible to us and others.

CONSERVATION VERSUS CONSUMPTION

Many ambitious CEOs and leaders take for granted their time and energy as they consume it liberally in the pursuit of goals. It is important to be more mindful about what you consider most important and commensurate of your time and energy.

TRAINING FOR THE RIGHT RACE

In life and other long-distance endurance events, success is about preparing and making the right sacrifices. The levels of sacrifice and preparation vary depending on what race you're running. Oftentimes, ambitious CEOs and other leaders underestimate the race they are running in and it causes them to struggle.

REFLECTIONS:

Some people would define a better family goal as spending more time together. Think about how you define success surrounding your personal or family goals?

On the next page is a copy of our goal matrix or you can download a pdf from www.peoplestretch.com/enduranceexecutive/goalmatrix. Please take a look at it and fill it out so you can get organized around your goals.

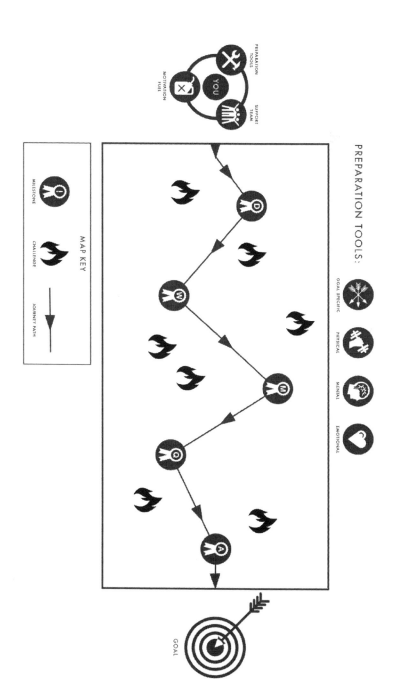

Chapter 4

SUPPORT IS MORE THAN "YES" MEN

I have worked with many CEOs who have no shortage of big, challenging goals like those we mentioned in the previous chapter. They struggle with a sense of isolation when there is no one to offer them support, encouragement, or accountability as they pursue these goals. In many cases, these CEOs are used to giving support, but struggle to accept it from others. Powerful leaders tend to surround themselves with people who share their values, and will execute their wishes.

When considering who you want to surround yourself with, finding like-minded supporters is key. Those people need to have a similar purpose and mindset. The challenge, however, is when those around you should be saying "no," but instead they say, "yes." That happens for a variety of different reasons, such as when one does not feel empowered to hold a leader accountable. They can also grow tired of offering advice that gets ignored. Find people who are supportive, but who will also push you to new levels. This will improve you as a person, as well as a professional.

Some of the participants in the Marine Corps Marathon trained together, as part of a running group. We took cabs from a store in Springfield, Virginia all the way to the start line, not far from the Arlington Cemetery. Among the group members were Jen and Joe, both lawyers for the army, who chased an elusive dream of running a sub-four-hour marathon time. The three of us completed many training runs and had a shared goal of "Four hours or bust." We joked about it, but little did we know what was to come.

When the race began, we stayed close. There's an important hill early in the race, during which you have to pace yourself. We ascended together. Running down the hill on mile four, we felt euphoric; it was the best mile of the race. As we went over a bridge and into Georgetown, Jen and Joe were running faster, so I thought, "At the six mile mark, I should pace myself and let them go ahead." I was able to see them for the next couple of miles before they left my sight.

Fast-forward to that grueling routine between miles 17 and 20. After hitting the wall, my strategy then involved thinking about composure, self-awareness, as well as passion, desire, and commitment. At every mile I reflected on my goals, and this tactic got me to the 14th Street Bridge. After crossing this bridge, I knew I had left D.C. and only had six miles left. On my way from Washington D.C. back to Virginia for the home stretch, I ran into Jen and Joe. I wasn't happy to see they had fallen on the same fate. It was mile 20 and the three of us were all struggling with major leg cramping, Jen in her calves and Joe in his quads. In rough shape, we limped in the rest of the way. We supported and encouraged each other, because we didn't want to walk, but we did want to finish the marathon.

Every mile or so, we stretched. Sometimes we stopped briefly; our longest stop was when we had about two miles left to go. After 24 miles of running, the whole body aches. All you do is try to stay focused on what that finish line will feel like when you cross it. The throbbing pain we experienced constantly distracted us, and made it difficult to keep our focus where it belonged. Together, we were able to get past the pain. We were ambitious. When we said, "four hours or bust," I'm not sure we gave enough thought to what "bust" might feel like.

A FALSE SENSE OF SECURITY

In my own work with CEOs, I've seen that there are a lot of ambitious people out there. As they grow professionally, success lulls them into a false sense of security. Despite having only one or two real confidantes, they do not believe they need a support team.

There are some inaccurate beliefs that hold leaders back from engaging with a team. For example, they've never needed help before, so why now? The reality is that the older we get, the more competing demands we face, which means we can run into some of the pitfalls we mentioned in previous chapters: falling short of goals, fear of failure and losing focus to distractions. Whether one works at a Fortune 500 company or a small business, from a day-to-day perspective, a lot of leaders are alienated, with no system of checks and balances.

WHAT DOES A SUPPORT TEAM NEED?

When I say "support team," I am referring to a group of peers who serve to both support a leader, as well as to coach him or her in decision-making and professional growth. Our supporters, especially if they are family members, will love us no matter what. Listed below are the three most important characteristics an endurance executive needs in support team members.

1. Encouragement: Specifically, encouragement towards goals. People like receiving praise, and we all need positive feedback. For the Endurance Executive, seeing accomplishments should satisfy that need for praise. It will not satisfy the need for encouragement that contributes to forward progress in goal achievement. Simple praise is different from encouragement, as one focuses on the immediate time, and the other looks toward the future.

Successful leaders set their sights on the future. When the journey gets difficult and there's a goal we're moving towards, we need reassurance that our goals are not far-fetched and that we can attain them if we continue moving in that direction. From mile 20 through the end of that race, it was the encouragement Jen, Joe, and I gave each other that made completing the race seem a little more real, more feasible. The togetherness made it easier to keep going. It would have been difficult to continue on in the pain of isolation.

2. Feedback: When I discussed my marathon debacle with my running coach, he gave me some honest feedback that I appreciated. For example, he told me that I went out too fast. While this was painful to hear, it was a good reminder of what not to do the next time I run a half or full marathon. In many cases, people don't get honest feedback when they don't give others permission to give them honest feedback.

We all need feedback on a consistent basis. The constructive way to think about this is, "I want my team/friend/family member to tell me why I did this right, or why I did it wrong." Feedback is not simply wanting to be told you're great at your job. Praise can be a type of feedback only when the "why" is explained. Criticism holds a great deal of value when presented in neutral, non-insulting language that defines why an individual did not live up to certain expectations, or perform as well as expected. Whether positive or constructive in nature, this type of feedback is appreciated by more people than a generic compliment of, "Hey, great job." Complements do not give Endurance Executives what they need to grow and achieve lofty goals.

3. Accountability: You have to ask your support team members to hold you accountable. Accountability is often misconstrued as being hard on someone else when they fall short, but that is inaccurate. Accountability starts with a clear understanding of the goals to which an individual is committing. If I'm committing to training five days a week and running 30 miles a week on average, I should expect more from my coach than a check-in to see if I completed my workouts. As an accountability support team member, his job is to hold me accountable for not just completing the workouts, but doing so in a way that will increase my ability to perform well. When I fall short, he must make sure I take ownership of shortcomings. Did I only train four out of five days? Did I do five days, but ran a shorter distance than the 30 miles I planned to do?

For an Endurance Executive, excellence in meeting commitments is an important motivational driver. It establishes and affirms the healthy mental and emotional dynamic of always moving towards goals. An Endurance Executive, leader, or CEO can get wonderful support from people who hold them accountable, whether it's from clients or being "managed up" by people who normally report to them.

Support teams, performance reviews and critiques are important tools for the CEO, but who's going to make sure the CEO seeks out this type of guidance? The answer is, it's largely the responsibility of the leader to seek that out. They can face real, detrimental challenges when they operate without accountability.

LEN FORKAS: FINDING THE WAY

Len Forkas is an Endurance Executive who understands the value of support. His commitment to his family carries over into not only his work, but into every race he runs. Len is married, a father of two, and the CEO of a growing Telecom company. What makes Len unique is his distinction as having competed in the hardest bike race in the world, the Race Across America. This race covers 3,000 miles in 12 days! I got a chance to interview Len and get to know his story, which he also captures in his book, *What Spins the Wheel: Leadership Lesson from our race for Hope.*

Len's story begins with a life proceeding as normal, until his son, Matt, was diagnosed with leukemia at the age of 9. It shook the family to the core. He recounts the first time going to the hospital for treatment. They were at Fairfax Hospital in Northern Virginia. Like many hospitals, Fairfax can be an antiseptic environment, seemingly a place of suffering more so than a place of recovery. Len's family knew they had to rally together to support Matt, and Len needed to be there for his son while also fulfilling all of his other demanding roles.

As anyone in this position can attest, supporting a loved one with cancer is a daunting task. The uncertainty you feel, combined with seeing someone you love in pain and witnessing their body change due to the chemotherapy, can be disheartening. Len came up with a great idea to help Matt cope with debilitating disease. He convinced Matt's school to put a video camera in his classroom, so Matt could stay connected with his friends and keep up in school.

It might not seem that innovative in 2015, but this took place in 2002, before Skype and Facetime were around. Len was able to wade through the bureaucracy of the Fairfax Country Public School system to get this approved and implemented in a short time period. While it took some tweaking, the end result was an amazing tool that helped Matt get through his treatment and see his friends. After connecting with his classmates, it was their interaction and encouragement that helped him stay positive about his situation.

Len had completed a number of 10K runs and Sprint Triathlons. In order to cope with the stress of Matt's sickness and all of his other responsibilities, Len remained active as a runner. During the spring of 2002, in the midst of his family's ordeal, Len signed up for the Marine Corps Marathon. The marathon was scheduled for October of 2002. Training for the marathon began around the same time Matt's treatment ended in July. Len gave much thought to the impact of the web camera on his son's morale and recovery. Could it help others? The answer was clear, and Len's charity, Hopecam (hopecam.org), was born.

The challenge was overcoming the cost of the project, at more than $1,100 per child. How could he come up with the money to help kids stay connected when they had cancer? This question dogged him throughout the training for his marathon. As September came and the race neared, Matt was able to return to school, a cancer survivor. All of his hair had grown in, and he was no longer bloated from steroids. His friends were happy to have him back.

The marathon came and went, but Len remained unable to answer the question—how could he come up with the money to help kids stay connected when they had cancer? In the aftermath of the race, a fellow marathoner pointed to a longer race, the JFK-50 Miler, and urged Len to consider running it. In an instant, Len saw an opportunity to not only run in that race, but to raise money for the fledgling idea. Len ran the first of many successful ultra-marathons, where he raised money for Hopecam. That progressed to Ironman Triathlons in 2007. You might recall this race from Kim Nelson's story in chapter one—an Ironman entails a 2.4 mile swim, a 112 mile bike ride, and a 26.2 mile run, all in a day's work.

Len did Ironman races to raise funds for the next few years until he was inspired to participate in the Race Across America at the end of 2011. He viewed this as a great opportunity to take fundraising to a completely different level. Previously, Len had raised tens of thousands of dollars in each race. For the 2012 Race Across America, on top of training for a 3,000 mile, 12 day bike race, he would set an ambitious fundraising goal: $150,000.

Len started doing some early preparation for this epic race and it became clear he would need to have an impressive cast of supporters to help him prepare and participate. He enlisted a team of 12 volunteers for the task. All were friends, or people who knew and connected with his goal. As in all of his other races, Len did not disappoint come race time. He finished in 10th place overall, out of 75 riders, and came in first in his age group. He also managed to raise $350,000!

Yes, it is possible that Len might be related to Superman, but he is as down to earth as it gets. I noticed a positive pattern in Len's behavior: He is particularly good at setting yearly goals. These goals have related to Hopecam and his duties as a father, husband, and CEO of a growing company.

Len does a great job of setting goals that are aligned with and complement each other. He has a big goal, but does not pursue it at the expense of his smaller goals. A common pitfall of many ambitious executives is focusing on big business goals, while personal and family lives are neglected. To Len's credit, he does an exceptional job of balancing his business needs with those of his personal life. He surrounds himself with a support system built from family members, colleagues, and other experienced athletes. These people provide guidance in all aspects of his life. Len's story embodies what an Endurance Executive is all about.

BUILDING THE TEAM

CEOs should ask themselves, "Who is best equipped to offer me encouragement, feedback, and accountability?" Some CEOs might ask for support from a past colleague who knows the environment in which the CEO operates, or they might ask a colleague who works in a different department of the same general industry. Support teams might include board members, family members, or friends. Who has the ability and—this is a harder question—who does the CEO trust to execute on those three very important functions (encouragement, feedback, and accountability) of a support team member?

It can take a CEO some time to assemble a support team. After you assemble a few members the process of developing and reviewing goals can begin. It's critical for the leader to eventually round out their team to five or six individuals, especially if they are prone to making long-term goals. If you can find four support team members relatively easily, then start there. Introduce your goals to them, so you can finalize the goals and start working. One of your goals can be to recruit a fifth and possibly sixth support team member.

People always ask, "How many people should be in a support team?" That number will vary from individual to individual, but I like the number five. Having five or six people takes the pressure off any one support team member to provide all of the needed guidance. I encourage Endurance Executives to make sure that support team members are socializing on a personal level, and establish good rapport between themselves, rather than merely participating as members of your support team. Through natural socialization between members, everyone takes turns offering encouragement, feedback, and discussing concerns surrounding accountability. That's the dynamic that an endurance executive needs.

Building a support team isn't all about social time, casual interaction, and friendship. As an Endurance Executive, you must always evaluate where you are with goal creation, and consistently take steps towards goal achievement. Support team members must understand and discuss your goals with you so that you're not developing them in isolation. We talked a little bit in the last chapter about the danger of setting goals in isolation. You can create the "rough drafts" of your goals alone, but you should not finalize them without discussing them with your support team. If your support team, upon review, thinks they're realistic and congruent with the bigger picture of your life and company, then they're appropriate to finalize and pursue.

If your support team thinks your goals are unrealistic, this is the first indication that you have not created a group composed of "yes men." You need support that challenges you and pushes back. It's not uncommon for CEOs to ignore their coaches' guidance. The Endurance Executive has to swallow his or her pride to avoid common pitfalls. If you want to receive support, first you have to listen.

Len Forkas's goal-setting abilities and commitment to his family are not the only features of Len's character that make him a great example of an Endurance Executive. He has found a way to combine both team-building and preparation in order to excel at his sport and in his company. In this book, we talk about how an Endurance Executive invests time to prepare in four different areas, including physical, emotional, mental, and goal specific preparation. For the Race Across America, Len did something that no other competitor did: He traveled with different members of his support team to see different parts of the race course.

These trips accomplished a multitude of goals. First, they helped Len and his team visualize the terrain, so they could plan accordingly. Second, it took the fear of the unknown out of play. Lastly, it gave his team time to develop a relationship that prepared them for the intensity of the race and the 12 days they spent working together toward a common goal.

TEAM MAINTENANCE: KEEPING (AND GROWING) YOUR SUPPORTERS

It is important to critically assess everything on an annualized basis, from your own performance, goal-setting, and progress, to the success of your support team. For more substantial long-term planning, evaluate these aspects your work every three to five years, in addition to annual reviews. Review the contributions of each support team member every year. If he or she contributed and gave you the encouragement, feedback, and accountability you needed throughout the year, keep him or her.

Keep in mind that the demands in people's lives can shift drastically year-to-year, and a support team member might find themselves suddenly lacking the time and energy needed to be there for you. Just because they participated for one year doesn't mean that they want to, or can participate for multiple years. It is helpful to get periodic recommitments from individuals on your support team, so they remain focused on delivering what the Endurance Executive asks of them.

CEOs may not realize how lonely they are. For a variety of reasons, they work in isolation, both literally and metaphorically. CEOs may spend long hours in private offices, having little contact with others. Even when they regularly work with a team, leaders can have serious trust issues. These trust issues lead to micromanagement and back-channeling, to keep tabs on the person(s) they do not trust. This type of bad behavior, gone unchecked, can get the best of any endurance executive or CEO. Having a strong team to evaluate and finalize goals, or to critique poor habits, is a boon to every Endurance Executive.

CHAPTER 4 SUMMARY

I have worked with many CEOs who have no shortage of big, challenging goals like those we mentioned in the previous chapter, but fail because they don't have the right (or enough) people supporting them. A key success factor of an Endurance Executive lies in the people supporting them, and whether those supporters are enough to help reach all of the Endurance Executive's goals.

A FALSE SENSE OF SECURITY

Success can lull CEOs and other leaders into a false sense of security, both in terms of confidence, as well as the need for support, coaching, feedback, etc.

WHAT DOES A SUPPORT TEAM NEED?

When I say "support team," I am referring to a group of peers who serve to both support a leader, as well as to coach him or her in decision-making and professional growth. The three key things a support team should provide are encouragement, feedback, and accountability.

BUILDING THE TEAM

CEOs should ask themselves, "Who is best equipped to offer me encouragement, feedback, and accountability?" Some CEOs might ask for support from a past colleague who knows the environment in which the CEO operates, or they might ask a colleague who works in a different department of the same general industry.

TEAM MAINTENANCE: KEEPING (AND GROWING) YOUR SUPPORTERS

It is important to critically assess your support team on an annualized basis, from your own performance, goal-setting, and progress, to the success of your support team. In some cases, an Endurance Executive will make changes to their support team in order to always have the best team to push them to succeed.

REFLECTIONS:

1. Can you think of a time when a support team could have made the difference in accomplishing a goal you previously have fallen short on?

2. Who can be on your support team? Will they be responsible for giving you encouragement, feedback and holding you accountable?

JOURNEY MAP:

PREPARATION TOOLS:

GOAL SPECIFIC   PHYSICAL   MENTAL   EMOTIONAL

GOAL

PREPARATION TOOLS

SUPPORT TEAM

YOU

MOTIVATION FUEL

MAP KEY

MILESTONE   CHALLENGE   JOURNEY PATH

Chapter 5

PREPARE FOR SUCCESS.....4 MUST HAVE TOOLS

After reuniting, Jen, Joe and I agreed that we would stay together for the remainder of the race. At mile 21, approaching the finish line, we all found a rhythm that felt great. We hit up a couple of tables for some M&Ms and Gatorade. We persevered even as the searing pain of the cramps pushed us to quit.

I dug deep into my stores of ambition, passion and desire in order to continue. In this moment of great discomfort, I promised myself that I would prepare differently next time. I made the commitment to change my habits so that I would never be in the same position again.

Preparation increases your chances for success. It's a mathematical probability not likely to shock anyone. Despite the overwhelming advantages of preparing, I still see many people who fail to do so. We're going to look at four areas of preparation(tools):

* Physical
* Mental
* Emotional
* Goal-Specific.

While none of the information I'm about to share will surprise a tried-and-true Endurance Executive, it's meant to provide insight for CEOs who are still growing their skill sets. Depending on where you are in your professional development, you will see different ways these areas of preparation are relevant to your life and work. As we grow older, we often ask ourselves, "Will I still be relevant?" Even something as natural as aging requires preparation, as you saw in our Cal Ripken story.

Ambitious individuals must think about physical well-being as well as mental, emotional, and goal-specific preparation, no matter how successful they've become. Needs change, people change and businesses grow and change. As I write this, I'm training to run a half marathon, which is far easier than training for a full marathon. It's not just twice as hard to train for a full marathon; it's also about two-and-a-half times as hard.

As we seek success at work, and in our personal and family lives, we must prepare across these three areas our lives like we've never prepared before. While you might not necessarily prepare for each area (mental, emotional, physical and goal-specific) every day, you have to prepare for all four when viewing life from the larger perspective.

YOUR SUPPORT TEAM WILL PREPARE YOU FOR SUCCESS

Remember in Chapter 4 how we discussed the nitty-gritty details of building your support team? The preparation phase is where that support team becomes so valuable. Develop a strategy identifying who will support you with which type of preparation. Select a team member who is aligned with each element of preparation. One person will serve as your accountability partner, while others focus on physical preparation, mental preparation, and so on. There should be a solid strategy behind how you choose to organize your support team, so that you are not only receiving feedback and guidance on your goal-setting, but you are also prepared for the challenges that you might face.

I'm blessed with some amazing support team members—people who are exponentially better runners and far more physically fit than I am. I also know people who are thoughtful, engage in meditation and mindfulness, and they can offer me great insight into emotional preparedness. Those who are strategic, who value planning and details, are the best to offer advice regarding mental preparation.

On the professional side, colleagues and fellow CEOs make great accountability partners. They can also help you with goal-specific preparation. Some well-known organizations offer peer-to-peer CEO executive forums, which are wonderful platforms for receiving developmental feedback. Acquiring a CEO support team member through one of these organizations is an easy way to find trustworthy peers for encouragement, feedback, and accountability.

When you look critically at these four areas of preparation, you cannot simply hand over to your team the responsibility to hold you accountable in all four areas, all at once. Being prepared means not only creating strategies, but, also building relationships with those who can guide you.

RUGGED TERRAIN, UNBREAKABLE SUPPORT

Alex Nemet seems like an ordinary CEO. We met at an entrepreneur conference sponsored by my company in October 2014. Alex's growing retail furniture business, Northeast Factory Direct, is based in Cleveland. He is happily married with kids. Pretty normal, right? However, while sitting next to each other, in conversation over dinner one night, I learned there was more to his story.

Alex is truly unique; in 2013, he raced in eight ultra-marathons of at least 100 miles each. Since 2005, he has run more than 30 ultra-marathons with distances of at least 100 miles. He was one of four runners to complete the Midwest Super Slam, which consisted of five 100-mile races, lasting from April through September of 2013. He completed the Super Slam with the lowest cumulative time, 135 hours.

In one of his early ultra-marathons, Alex tweaked his knee at mile nine of a 100-mile race! The pain progressively worsened over the course of the run, especially on downhill stretches. Two key factors enabled Alex to persevere. Primarily, he told himself that dropping out of the race was not an option; his commitment to finish was unbreakable. He would finish, even if it meant walking at times.

In addition, Alex also relied on his ability to focus on positive thoughts when the pain level spiked. He concentrated on the belt buckle he would receive for racing in this ultra-marathon. He has a drawer full of buckles, but this one in particular is special because of how difficult the race turned out to be.

Alex also discussed his experience at the 2009 Badwater Ultramarathon, as it represented a pivotal point in his personal journey. Badwater is one of the hardest races in the United States. Runners start at below sea level in California's Death Valley and traverse 124 miles, before arriving at the base of Whitney Portals. A winding road takes you from the bottom of the canyon to the base of Mt. Whitney, and at the end of the race is an 11-mile, 4,700-foot-high vertical climb to the top of Whitney Portals. A few years after Alex competed in Badwater, the racecourse was changed due to dangerous conditions—most notably, the 120-130 degrees Fahrenheit daytime temperatures in Death Valley.

During Badwater, Alex had a crew consisting of his 15-year-old daughter, Sam; his training partner and frequent co-race participant, Frank Fumich; and Aaron Ralston. Ralston is the climber that the movie *127 Hours* was based on, who amputated his own arm to dislodge himself after he became trapped in a fallen rock formation.

The support of Alex's pregnant wife, Julie, also factored into the pre-race excitement. Unfortunately, one week prior to the race, Alex and Julie were told that the baby's heartbeat was undetectable, which indicated they'd lost the child. It was a crushing blow, but Julie insisted Alex run, due to all the planning and training that had gone into preparing him for the challenge. She also thought it would help him cope with the loss.

The first 25 miles of the race seemed fairly easy. Alex went out a little fast, but he felt good about the start. By Mile 40, he started to struggle, as his body told him he wasn't taking in enough salt. Luckily, Frank paced him for the next 25 miles to help him through this low point. The practice of pacing is when a crew member runs with a participant for a period of time in order to provide support. Teamwork got him through that low point, but there were more obstacles to come. At Mile 70, as the sun was coming up, an F14 fighter jet on a Death Valley training run flew overhead. It felt like the plane was close, so the noise and feel shocked Alex into a greater state of alertness, providing a much needed wave of energy.

At the next aid station, Sam gave her father a cell phone and said her mother wanted to speak to him. Julie gave him the best news he had ever received over the phone. After consulting a different physician for a second opinion, their baby's heartbeat had been found. The child would survive. At that moment, tragedy turned into a source of inspiration. A wave of emotion pulsed through Alex and he broke down in tears. Knowing he had to capitalize on this wave of energy, he resumed the race.

At Mile 85, struggling again, Alex reached another aid station. He still had another 50 miles to go and was not feeling like he could complete it. He looked at his crew and felt a sense of defeat creeping in. As the pain and exhaustion screamed through this body, Alex became angry with himself for even considering defeat. He restarted the race by listening to music and running as hard as he could. He started to pass people, and each one he passed made him feel stronger.

Alex's laser-sharp focus indicated to his crew that he was on a mission to finish. He reached the base of the Whitney Portals, the last 11-mile leg of the race, and stopped there long enough to take a Vicodin and drink a Red Bull. From that point, Aaron paced him up the hill and Alex finished the race! And he ended up running the fifth fastest leg for the last 50 miles!

The experience was a roller coaster ride of emotional and physical agony, followed by great joy and ultimate victory. Alex didn't just run the Badwater; the race represented a rebirth of hope, for himself and his family. It meant overcoming obstacles in the face of tragedy.

When Nemet reflected on the race during our interview, he was adamant that he would not have made it without the combination of his intensive preparation and the hard work of his support team. The support he received from his wife, in spite of her misdiagnosed miscarriage, contributed significantly to his success.

He also credits the team at his business for allowing him to focus on preparing for the race and providing great support to him. He could race comfortably knowing that a trustworthy team would take care of his business and keep it running smoothly. Despite the trials and tribulations of Badwater, Alex persevered and was able to record another memorable moment in his journey.

In both sports and business, one can never underestimate the power of a strong team. The endurance executive surrounds him or herself with family, friends and people who have the ability to encourage, and provide feedback and accountability—on the racecourse, and in the boardroom.

SKILLS TO LIVE (AND WORK) BY

I reflected a great deal on how I could have prepared differently for the marathon. I thought about times when I was successful as a CEO and how preparation played a role in contributing to that success. I used my own experiences and way of thinking to work with my CEO clients. I noticed that, even with a support team, we can miss out leveraging them fully. This is often because people are at different levels of maturity in developing communication skills.

Teams are both built upon, and destroyed by, quality of communication skills. It can be especially difficult to have conversations about failure and making behavior changes. Members who are not as far along in developing communication skills may struggle to find the right words to discuss shortcomings, or fall into the previously mentioned trap of becoming "yes men."

An unprepared support team cannot provide guidance, or push a leader toward better overall preparation. As an Endurance Executive invests time and energy into his or her support team, certain skills need to be developed. These skills help an Endurance Executive get more out of a well-prepared support team. This results in better focus and strengthened commitment toward the pursuit of goals.

PAST FAILURE

In order for success to exist, so must failure. We have to understand what failure looks like, before we can truly prepare for success. We must also be open about failure—face it, talk about it with our support teams, and understand that failure can be an opportunity for positive growth. As we discussed in previous chapters, the fear of failure can be a good thing if it is a managed and balanced aspect of one's ambition. When you understand the implications that surround your potential for failure in certain goals or pursuits, you can learn a lot.

Preparation creates learning opportunities. I learned a great deal from hitting the wall so early in my marathon. Difficult experiences have taught me many things throughout my life and career. When my dad promoted me to CEO, it was not uncommon for me to make a mistake every quarter. Sometimes, I made a bad decision with a channel distributor or about how to treat an end user customer. I made mistakes regarding other employees. Failure was not fun, but it was necessary. Whether it's a mistake at work or in a personal relationship, it's critical for us to leverage our support team and be able to talk about failure in an open way.

THE SOFT SKILLS OF COMMUNICATION

I try to work daily on improving the soft skills I need to interact with my support team. I want to communicate better, a skill most of us will hone throughout our lives. A lot of people make the mistake of thinking they're great communicators. No matter how great your ideas, they'll get you nowhere if you cannot articulate them well. Endurance Executives are in a perpetual state of developing and refining their communication skills. They should always be working on how they communicate with individuals, teams, and customers. That expanded skill set will bleed over into family life and personal relationships.

Try to communicate directly, transparently, and respectfully. I've worked extremely hard on developing my language and improving how I express ideas. When we communicate directly, we go straight to the person of concern. An employee should not hear praise or criticism "through the grapevine." It should be heard through personalized contact.

Transparency in communication entails saying exactly what you mean. Respectful communication requires mindfulness of how the other person feels, and staying conscious of the language used. When you're communicating directly, respectfully, and in a transparent fashion, you're also sharing how you feel and what your motivation is in the communication.

I've been extremely impressed by CEOs at all levels, from Fortune 500 companies to small businesses. I've seen people outside the corporate world communicate in amazing ways. I have been wowed by doctors in hospitals, as well as by preachers and pastors who convey a message of faith to their parishioners. People don't always understand intuitively that you have to be mindful of how people feel during verbal communications. Sometimes they struggle with communicating transparently while also being thoughtful. Taking the time to do that can be difficult in our fast-paced world.

If you want to be your best, whether you're communicating with a spouse, friend, child, client, or employee, you have to be able to communicate in a way that is direct, transparent, and respectful. Building this skill set is a lifelong process. You are never too old or too smart to become a better communicator.

LISTENING

Another important soft skill is listening. Many CEOs have been accused of being "tone deaf" toward people's needs. Listening is not just about hearing what is literally being said, but also tuning in empathically and trying to understand the tone of the message. I didn't always do that in the past, and I work with CEOs today who don't. However, I admire excellent listeners. My wife will laugh when she reads this, but I believe females are much better at listening than males. I acknowledge my shortcoming and work on it every day—some days more successfully than others.

THE SATURATION POINT

Distraction is an important pitfall to avoid when it comes to goals. Everyone has to be aware of what their saturation point is. The "saturation point" occurs when an individual's mind or body is overwhelmed, so that they can no longer process what's coming at them. An Endurance

Executive must be able to realize when he or she has reached the saturation point, especially with all the stimuli of today's world. Every moment, we are surrounded by calls, texts, social media, emails, people walking into the office, our kids' needs, and our spouses asking questions.

Reaching the saturation point is a great indicator that one has failed in preparation. In this situation, take a look at how you're preparing for your days and weeks, then make adjustments. Preparation means anticipating distractions and curtailing them. For some people, working from home is difficult, because of the chaos of family life. They must plan, for example, to go into the office on days their children are home from school. A certain chatty coworker might take up too much of your time with conversation, so be prepared to keep talk with that individual short, but polite.

Maybe you tackled too much and the stress got to you, or you're late because you allowed a meeting to go on too long. There are a variety of different reasons for reaching your saturation point. Always mindful of strategy and preparation, the Endurance Executive does not reach that saturation point. Preparation is preventative medicine at its finest.

KATHY LANIER: A COMMITMENT TO LIFELONG LEARNING

In writing this book and selecting Endurance Executives to interview or reference, I wanted to select one who wasn't an endurance athlete, but who embodies all of the characteristics of one. That particular person is Cathy Lanier. Although I live in Northern Virginia, I am a huge fan of Washington, D.C. Police Chief, Cathy Lanier. Her story is amazing, and exemplifies the commitment we see in the lives of Endurance Executives. She dropped out of school during ninth grade and became a single mom when she was only 15 years old. After a divorce from her son's father, she moved back in with her mother and began working two jobs in order to complete her GED. In 1990, at the age of 23, Cathy Lanier joined the Metropolitan Police of D.C.

Lanier was attracted to a career as a public servant because her brother worked for the police department and her father was a fireman. She also saw an opportunity to further her education through the tuition reimbursement programs offered to police officers. She took advantage of those incentives in order to finish her bachelor's degree, as well as a Master's of Management from Johns Hopkins University. From the Naval Postgraduate School, Lanier received an additional Master's in National Security Studies. She achieved all of this while working full time!

Lanier was named captain in 1999, and rose to the position of chief in 2007, at the age of 40. Taking into consideration her hard work and focus on long-term achievement, it is no wonder she experienced such a meteoric rise. In researching and speaking with Chief Lanier, what stood out most was how she lives and embodies the habits and work ethic of an Endurance Executive.

Her commitment to continued education and personal growth for her career has been impressive. The knowledge she gained from completing two master's degrees distinguishes her from many of her peers, and helped in her ascension to top ranking positions in the MPDC. In addition, while heading the special operations division, she traveled abroad to Israel. This provided opportunities to learn more about how other countries are dealing with terrorism. She was exposed to radically different ideas, perspectives, and tactics used by the Israelis. Lanier credits that trip for influencing many of her important professional decisions when she returned to the States. She implemented versions of these ideas in her work with the MPDC.

As an Endurance Executive, Lanier is able to recognize when she is reaching her saturation point. In a city like D.C., the press and politics can get the best of you, and she has learned how to manage both. On the press side, she has found that it is important to avoid "no comment" responses to tough questions. Chief Lanier tries to always give the media some information; she recognizes that members of the press are just people, trying to do their jobs.

In terms of politics, it can be difficult negotiating with unions that often have negative responses to MPDC leadership. She is quick to acknowledge that while politics can feel brutal, it is not a personal issue. Learning to avoid taking business and political matters personally has helped Lanier manage conflicts in an objective, constructive way, while keeping her own feelings out of these matters.

One of Chief Lanier's impressive qualities is her ability to project and focus on goals that will continue to develop her own future in leadership. She does this by undertaking goal-specific preparation for challenges that might occur further down the road. Back in 2012, Lanier worked on a five-year study, leveraging economic data to do resource planning, which required asking for funding for more police officers and equipment.

Thanks to growth in D.C.'s economy over the study period, the nighttime population became as large as the daytime population, which has been largely driven by the federal workforce. New housing and a proliferation of nightlife, bars, and sport venues encouraged more people to stay out (and contribute to the local economy) later into the night. Thus, the need for an active nighttime police force increased. Lanier used the data from the study to justify her need for appropriate staffing changes in evening security measures in certain parts of the city. Oftentimes, what drives police force expansion is a rise in crime, but the crime rate has remained in check on Chief Lanier's watch.

To keep it that way, she needed to be proactive and offer a different perspective on her city's constantly changing needs. Doing a study was a great example of how her preparation has helped her stay ahead of the crime. Furthermore, if we look at how she has consistently returned to school for her undergraduate and master's degree, or traveled abroad to continue her learning, her commitment to preparation is unprecedented for a police officer. They are not obligated to complete advanced degrees, or travel, as part of their jobs!

Lanier had a vision: She wanted to be successful over a long period of time and she has continually pushed herself in different areas to prepare her for continued growth. As of the writing of this book, there are rumors Cathy might run for Mayor in the future...

CHAPTER 5 SUMMARY

Preparation increases your chance of success. You cannot cut corners if you want to consistently be successful. An Endurance Executive is committed to his or her success and views preparation as "tools." The four must-have tools of preparation are:

* Physical
* Mental
* Emotional
* Goal-Specific

YOUR SUPPORT TEAM WILL PREPARE YOU FOR SUCCESS

The preparation phase is where that support team becomes so valuable, in that they ensure the Endurance Executive invests the appropriate amount of time into each type of preparation in order to be successful. Many CEOs and other leaders don't have accountability when it comes to preparation—a contributing reason for why their performance struggles.

SKILLS TO LIVE (AND WORK) BY

Even with the right support team, a CEO can fail if they don't have the right conversations with their team. It all starts with communication skills, which an Endurance Executive always believes are important to develop, regardless of whether they're an introvert or extrovert.

PAST FAILURE

In order for success to exist, so, too, must failure. We have to understand what failure looks like before we can truly prepare for success.

THE SOFT SKILLS OF COMMUNICATION

Endurance Executives are perpetually refining the soft skills needed to interact with their support team. They want to communicate better, a skill most people need to hone throughout their lives.

LISTENING

Another important soft skill is listening. Many CEOs have been accused of being "tone-deaf" toward people's needs. This is part of an Endurance Executive's perpetual work on honing communications skills.

THE SATURATION POINT

This is when a CEO's mind experiences "burn-out" and they can no longer process as effectively what is coming at them, causing them to make bad decisions and behave erratically.

REFLECTIONS

"What do I need to do to succeed?" is a great question to ask yourself as you're working towards your goals. You might also need to consider "How do I not fail?" Your success will hinge upon what you do to prepare.

1. How will you develop your 4 preparation tools: physical, mental, emotional, and goal-specific preparation?
2. Where do you fall in the pendulum of preparation? Do you under- or over-prepare?
3. Of the four areas of preparation that we've discussed (physical, mental, emotional, and goal specific) where do you think you most need to improve?

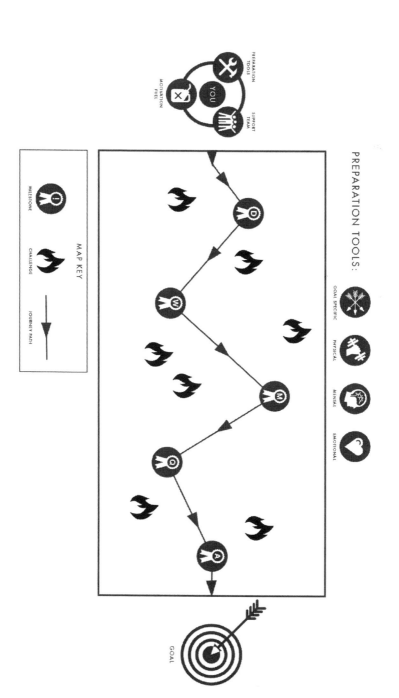

Chapter 6

GOAL-SPECIFIC PREPARATION

In the previous chapter, we identified preparation as a significant factor in becoming an Endurance Executive. In this chapter, we will focus on *goal-specific preparation*. Goal-specific preparation is the sum total of everything you are doing to help you move into your next stage of growth. A lot of different requirements—including physical, emotional, and mental energy—go into properly training oneself for a specific goal. Whether you want to make the jump from a VP to C-level—or be as capable a CEO of a $100M company as you were when it was $10M— there are many goal-specific preparation techniques that will help you achieve your goal.

Goal-specific preparation proves most challenging for many of the executives I've had a chance to work with, mostly because they have not spent time planning for their company's next stage of growth. It can be difficult to foresee where one's own personal evolution will take the business, and sometimes CEOs don't have the experience to make accurate predictions about the future. Of course, sometimes outside circumstances can alter one's path to the next level of personal and corporate growth.

An endurance CEO might decide to learn a new language one year, and in the next try to learn a new computer programming language. Maybe the goal is to improve one's extemporaneous speaking, or any other number of hobbies and self-actualizing pursuits.

How successful an endurance CEO is in accomplishing these goals depends on a number of things, including having access to support, be it group learning with support team members, or recruiting a more dedicated resource like a personal executive coach. This entire process, from making the plan to finding resources to help you accomplish it, shows an Endurance CEO's commitment to reaching their next stage of personal growth.

AN ENDURANCE EXECUTIVE ON PREPARATION AND SUCCESS

Patrick Sweeney is an Endurance Executive I had the chance to meet and interview for this book. He is a great example of someone who demonstrates commitment towards goal-specific preparation.

Patrick Sweeney is accustomed to success. He competed in the Olympic trials in 1996, and afterwards went on to start four groundbreaking technology companies, with three successful exits. His latest project, Dwinq, is a social media platform that helps large companies transform consumers into brand champions.

In addition to starting and running tech companies, Patrick has competed in his fair share of adventure races. In 2014, he set his sights on the Iditarod Trail Invitational, the coldest, longest endurance bike race in the world. Spanning 350 miles over five days, the Invitational takes place in Alaska during the month of February. Day temperatures regularly dip below freezing, and can drop to -40 degrees Fahrenheit at night. This is the same trail on which the famed Iditarod sledding race takes place.

Riders push their bodies for 17 or 18 hours each day, braving the elements with hopes of finishing the race in less than six days. Patrick's training and goal-specific preparation routine was impressive. He highlighted three key things that help him train at his best:

1. **VO2 Max:** Also known as maximum oxygen consumption, VO2 Max calculates the maximum rate of oxygen consumed during exercise by comparing one's resting heart rate is against their heart rate while vigorously performing an exercise. This number helps to calibrate training in the right zone so that athletes avoid the "grey zone." The grey zone is whenever a person, so focused on training a specific set of muscles, trains that muscle group either too quickly or too slowly, reducing the effectiveness of his or her training. Knowing VO2 Max helps prevents over- or under-training.

2. **Blood Analysis:** Overall, blood analysis gives great feedback on the quality your diet and whether you are over-training. According to Patrick Sweeney and his doctors, a key thing to watch out for is a Vitamin D deficiency, which affects over 2,000 genes in our bodies. The function of Vitamin D is important in regulating exercise-related inflammation, immunity and bone density. More than 40 percent of the U.S. population is deficient, and the National Institutes of Health (NIH) has even named it a worldwide epidemic that affects calcium metabolism and bone health.

3. **Body Fat Analysis:** Power-to-weight ratio can be a crucial number for endurance athletes. They can improve their VO2 max by staying aware of this number, to determine whether a reduction in body weight is needed to improve performance. Patrick explains that improvement is more important than reaching a final number.

Patrick's goal-specific preparation for the bike race was amazing. He did acclimatization training in Chamonix, France. He trained outside in the cold to encourage vaso-dilatation, for increased blood flow to extremities to help ready his body for the rigors of riding a mountain bike through snow during the Alaskan winter. He credits preparation and training as important elements that helped him stay in the race.

Another key factor that got Patrick through the hardest part of the race was staying close to another rider going from Rainy Pass to Rohn, the challenging part of the race. In this stage of the race, the riders ascend a peak 3,167 feet above sea level, but given that timing factors into the event, Patrick had to do the ascent at night. It proved harrowing, but since he was able to do it with someone else, it gave him the needed support to get through a grueling point. Sweeney eventually camped out for a couple of hours after reaching the summit, because his body could not go any further.

Patrick came close to disaster when he took a wrong turn near the end of the race. This took him 5 miles and two hours off-course, after four days and more than 340 miles of racing. He referred to this mistake as "purgatory." While it felt demoralizing to backtrack and pick up the trail, knowing he was near the finish line allowed him to stay focused. Patrick found the trail and finished the race with a time of four days and 10 hours. Amazingly, he completed the race on just over six hours of sleep during the entirety of the four-and-a-half day race.

Endurance Executives will inevitably be faced with challenges that feel like summiting a mountain, or getting lost along the way to the finish line. The key is to stay calm and focused on one's goals to get through those difficult periods. This sense of struggle, overcome through perseverance, is a consistent theme in stories of Endurance Executives.

COMMITMENT MEANS DIFFERENT THINGS TO DIFFERENT PEOPLE

Commitment can mean different things to different people. For the sake of our discussion, we will define it as what you are reasonably and ethically prepared to do to become successful. Any type of personal achievement requires a commitment of time and resources in order to move forward.

Many CEOs and leaders are unaware of the investment and sacrifice required to build a life and career based on constant growth. If commitment isn't maintained or increased over time, growth plateaus. Upward mobility stagnates. The hardest part is being aware of when one has reached this point. Luckily, the right support team can help you take notice.

Educating your support team is critical. They must understand the importance of making commitments and staying focused on your preparation. The "right" level of support team interaction will vary from individual to individual, but what is most important is that they are there when needed most to provide knowledge and feedback.

My goal-specific preparation for my sub-four hour marathon goal did not include identifying all of the goal-specific variables. I could have impacted my potential for improved performance prior to the race by engaging my support team in the right way for this specific goal. Patrick Sweeney's goal-specific variables, especially body fat analysis, were the same ones I could have managed better for my own race.

By looking more carefully, I would have realized I needed to lose as much as 10 pounds for optimal performance. I also trained in the "grey zone," as I did a lot of my long runs at a fast pace. The purpose of long runs is to run slow so that you can build endurance. I didn't understand the impact of the "grey zone" and its long-term effects, and because of this I was not adequately prepared for the race.

I had my support team encouraging me to persevere through training and ensuring I didn't miss workouts, but I didn't have anyone with a focused marathon background. Having someone with a background like Patrick's could have potentially saved me from myself, in terms of making me aware of the benefits of running slower and losing another 10 pounds prior to the race. It is critical to have the right individuals on your support team, who understand what role they play in your success.

NURTURING THE ENDURANCE EXECUTIVE

Working with clients on goal-specific preparation, I have learned there are behaviors an Endurance Executive always tries to nurture within themselves. The first is staying to stay curious and learn. An unquenchable thirst for knowledge serves the Endurance Executive well. When an individual is always looking to gain new knowledge, it pushes them to grow as professionals and individuals. I've seen this curiosity in many of the successful CEOs I've worked with or studied, as well as in myself.

In one of my worst moments, after my mom died, my natural curiosity dropped for a time. During this time, there were also conflicts in both my professional and private life. My executives weren't performing well, and I struggled to understand why. At home, my two-year-old son, Jack, was diagnosed with PDDNOS (Pervasive Developmental Disorder Not Otherwise Specified).

Overcoming both challenges became goals of mine, and I didn't have enough information in my own knowledge bank to deal with both. Thanks to the support of everyone around me, this depression didn't last long. This need to overcome challenges reignited my passion for learning. I had two great reasons to consume a dramatic amount of information about psychology, behavioral science, developmental psychology, and neuroscience. I was fortunate I was able to get back into my overall learning journey.

Over the years, I've encountered people who felt they had reached a point where they'd done enough professional learning. In most of those situations, they also felt they'd reached a career plateau, but they were unable to understand how those two things are related. Learning stagnation is a huge contributing factor to hitting the wall.

Another area on which Endurance Executives always continue to work is their communication skills. When I consider the all-time greatest CEOs, they all have in common a strong ability to communicate well. Great communication skills, however, are challenging to develop, and may take many years of concentrated effort.

It's easy for extroverted CEOs to feel that they're great communicators, but oftentimes these same leaders are likely to have poor listening skills. As a CEO becomes more successful, listening to others is a skill that often begins to wane. Success can strengthen confidence, but it can also discourage leaders from listening to others when there is dissention. It can also cause a leader to not heed their support group if the group is trying to hold them accountable on a sensitive issue. Another challenge extroverts in particular face is long-windedness in delivering their messages. Fortune 100 CEOs have learned how to strike a balance between being succinct and articulate when speaking with others. We can find a great example of this style in Jack Welch, whom I was fortunate enough to hear speak on TV and in person.

As the legendary CEO of GE, he presided over unprecedented growth for a company of that size. He was charismatic and able to motivate many, and his skillful communication style positively influenced his work and life. He does an amazing job of providing thorough explanation, without belaboring the point. An example of his great communication skills can be found in some of his quotes; I've included my two favorites:

"Control your own destiny or someone else will."
"When you were made leader, you weren't given a crown,
you were given the responsibility to bring out the best in others."

Introverted CEOs, on the other hand, tend to be naturally good listeners, but can be succinct to a fault. Some struggle with articulating their ideas to their teams, because introverts may find connecting with people to be a challenge. Both of these characteristics—personal connection, and lacking explanation in conversation—can be corrected over time. To do so requires great effort on the part of the CEO, especially when they are introverted or communication skills don't come naturally.

Many CEOs don't think they need to improve as communicators. They carry an underlying belief they are good enough to get what they want and need. However, this is a self-limiting belief, as even the best communicators still have room to grow. Different generations have unique ways of communicating, and in a large organization employing people of all ages, these differences must be understood for smooth operation. Those who work with multinational companies may spend their careers networking with people from cultures around the world and must become comfortable with unfamiliar customs in communication. This is a lifelong process.

A great line of questions to ask yourself, or someone you are supporting:

1. What kind of impact would it make if you were a better communicator at work?

2. What kind of impact would this have on your relationships with friends and family? Your spouse? Your children?

Asking these types of questions will challenges a CEO by encouraging them to look at their communication skills from a new perspective. In my work with CEOs, I have seen direct correlation between success in the C-Suite, and how much time and energy leaders invested into improving their communication skills. An Endurance Executive knows that improving communication will always be part of goal-specific preparation for business. Poor communication skills alienate others, and one cannot succeed without connected guidance and support.

Goal-specific preparation can cut into time spent with family, friends, and personal interests. In many cases, numerous hours of work invested into goal-specific preparation provide only incremental gains. However, when all the same gains are added up, over the course of a career and lifetime, we see they are not so small. The long-term effects are huge.

Kim Nelson, the Tri-athlete CEO from Toronto whom we met in Chapter One, has seen goal-specific preparation pay dividends on the racecourse, and in growing her company. Investing time in goal-specific preparation is part of a process that has helped her compete in over 18 Ironman triathlons and run businesses exceeding $150M in revenue. Kim has willingly sacrificed her time to position herself for continued success.

CHAPTER 6 SUMMARY

This type of preparation focuses on the goal itself and, in many cases, involves acquiring a new skill or improving an existing one due to the demands of the goal. An example of acquiring a new skill is learning a new language; if an Endurance Executive wants to work abroad it would increase their chances of getting an assignment or job.

Improving an existing skill in goal-specific preparation requires two steps: assessment of skill, and effort to improve. For example, an Endurance Executive could get an assessment from a communications specialist on their public speaking skills, and they can continue to improve on them if their new goal requires it.

COMMITMENT MEANS DIFFERENT THINGS TO DIFFERENT PEOPLE

Commitment towards a goal can be difficult to maintain with all of the competing priorities and demands on a leader's time. A blind spot for many CEOs and other leaders who struggle at some point in their career is how committed they are in a given situation, based on their ability to balance that with all of their other commitments. This is where a support team can make a huge difference by educating the Endurance Executive on the goal-specific preparation needed to succeed and helping maintain the executive's commitment toward the most important goals.

NURTURING THE ENDURANCE EXECUTIVE

Working with clients on goal-specific preparation, I have learned that certain behaviors help a CEO or other leader nurture the Endurance Executive within themselves. Curiosity and learning are two such behaviors that help stimulate growth. Curiosity can lead an Endurance Executive to explore new ideas that drive creativity, success in strategy, and the desire to learn new skills. Curiosity leads to learning, a practice an Endurance Executive is always engaging in, as they see learning as a key part of their journey. Every goal offers the opportunity for goal-specific preparation that will help one learn new skills or acquire knowledge that will enrich their life.

REFLECTIONS:

1. What are some goal-specific variables you should be working on in respect to your important goals?
2. Does your support team offer any insight or support regarding your goal-specific preparation?
3. How does your curiosity and desire to learn compare to when you were 25 or 30?
4. Where do you fall in terms of your listening and communication skills?

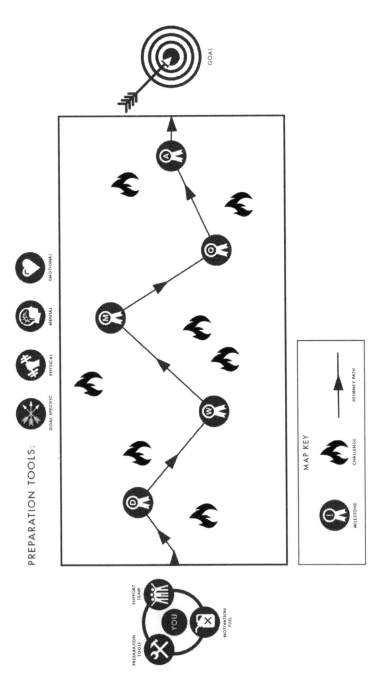

JOURNEY MAP:

PREPARATION TOOLS:

GOAL SPECIFIC · PHYSICAL · MENTAL · EMOTIONAL

GOAL

PREPARATION TOOLS · SUPPORT TEAM · YOU · MOTIVATION FUEL

MAP KEY

MILESTONE · CHALLENGE · JOURNEY PATH

Chapter 7

MENTAL PREPARATION

When people hear the term "mental preparation," it conjures up an image of an event unfolding toward a desired outcome. Many leaders I work with, usually due to of lack of time or commitment, struggle to find time for the preparation needed to ensure desired outcomes.

When mental preparation does occur, it resembles a check list or agenda. On this agenda, individuals organize their thoughts about processes that will enable them to problem-solve. What's generally missing from this equation is identification of the desired outcome, and alternatives to be considered if the desired outcome isn't obtained. This semblance of preparation, in the form of note-taking and list-making will be done, in most cases, over a short period of time. It creates the illusion of preparation, but can be incomplete.

Inadequate mental preparation for the marathon led to a painful experience during my race. I thought the only thing I had to mentally prepare for was running on-pace, uphill, in miles two and three, avoiding going too fast due to the adrenaline of the start of the race. I did a good job of preparing for that, but a poor job preparing for everything else. What surprised and got the best of me was how fast I ran down the hill on Spout Run Parkway, and over the Key Bridge into Georgetown.

I had not mentally prepared to pace myself when running downhill, and before I knew it, I was over two minutes ahead of my pace. I had never run a marathon before, and that contributed to my ignorance. Ignorance is not always bliss, and boy, did I pay for it when I hit the wall at mile 14.

As Jen, Joe and I painfully persevered in the last three or four miles, I vowed that when it comes to what is most important to me, I will mentally prepare and visualize how things will go from start to finish. If you want to perform at an elite level with consistency, it requires a dramatic amount of mental preparation over an extended period of time.

HEALTHY SKEPTICISM

A healthy sense of skepticism is an important tool to carry in your mental preparation toolkit. We all love to think things will go as planned. In an ideal world, the marathon would have gone as planned. Healthy skepticism might have helped me prepare for hitting the wall at an earlier point in the race, or to start out slower. In business, what our plan looks like is only the first step. Taking that plan from paper to mental visualization of how it will unfold is important.

A lot of CEOs plan meetings carefully. They consider what they're going to talk about, their presentation at the meeting, and their actions, but rarely about what happens if these meetings do not go as planned. A lot of times, leaders are more focused on ensuring the delivery of their message is appropriate and well-spoken, than they are the desired outcome from delivering the message in the first place.

A pitfall that gets the best of CEOs (present company included) is unwavering trust in their own problem-solving expertise. Believing they have all the skills necessary to solve every potential problem, between themselves and their team members, will prevent development of that healthy sense of skepticism. It also creates the belief that complex problems can be solved on the fly. We should always ask ourselves if we really have the resources to solve every possible problem when it arises, then follow up with, "What if we can't solve it?"

Mental preparation includes visualizing how we would like situations to go, then thinking about contingency planning. You might feel great the morning of, or the night before, but that still doesn't mean you shouldn't go through contingency planning. This type of planning is like an umbrella: You don't always need it when you bring it with you, but every time you have to use it, you feel glad you were prepared. This doesn't mean you shouldn't visualize the ideal outcome as well. Imagining the perfect ending is the starting point for mental preparation. To further buoy your contingency planning, you should challenge the orthodoxy of how possible problems are commonly solved. Relying on commonly accepted solutions reduces innovation and creativity, two important features of successful long-term problem-solvers.

I'm going to credit this line of thinking to a mentor of mine, New York Times Best Selling Author, Dan Pink. He decided to write about a project that my brother and I did in memory of our mom. As fellow Washington D.C. natives, we quickly built a supportive relationship. In his book, *Drive*, he talks about challenging the accepted rationales behind why we do what we do. In many cases, challenging the orthodoxy can expose examples of counterintuitive thinking and improve the likelihood of positive outcomes.

A good example of counterintuitive thinking is underestimating demand for a product launch, which can lead to running out of stock. One of the most popular wine brands in the United States, Yellow Tail, from Australia, started small before it grew, in only one year, to over one million cases sold annually! The winery only started with 20,000 cases because they were confident that demand for the initial vintage would outstrip supply. They had no idea it would do so in only two weeks. The frenzy for slickly packaged, underpriced wines from Australia continued to outstrip supply for the next 12 months, as the winery could not keep up with the demand.

Another challenge to mental preparation for many CEOs is they often fill up their schedules with too many responsibilities. It starts at the beginning of the day when a CEO thinks they are preparing for the day by creating a long task list. They may call it "planning," but in all actuality, they are planning to stretch themselves too thin. Instead of a million tiny tasks, plan for success and/or obtaining the ideal outcome on the most important tasks on your schedule. Some people who manage complex scenarios at work, or serve in constantly-changing industries, need to invest more time in order to avoid blind spots. They should visualize ideal outcomes, and anticipate a reasonable number of contingencies for each event. Complex industries need complex contingency plans.

With technology and other trends changing how we work, year to year, what worked last year might not work this year. For example, there has been a recent proliferation of people who are not money-motivated. Pink wrote about this in his book, *Drive*, and it has forced leaders to re-evaluate how to motivate people. If you need someone to do something for you, monetary gain may not be the controlling lever it used to be. Find other alternatives, like paid time off or additional free training, to use as the new motivational levers.

Success and experience, while great attributes, can also turn into pitfalls when it comes to mental preparation. Our confidence is influenced by our performance in past events and previous experiences. This confidence can cause us to underestimate how much preparation is needed for a particular situation. Exceptionally successful CEOs can become vulnerable to this dynamic. A perfect example is the CEO of British Petroleum, Tony Hayward. He was delivering a great result relative to his competitors one minute, and the next minute went into a career tailspin over an impulsive comment he made on CNN during the Gulf Oil Spill TV coverage.

He commented, "I'm sorry. We're sorry for the massive disruption it's caused their lives. There's no one who wants this over more than I do. **I'd like my life back.**" He chose these words, rather than demonstrating stronger concern or empathy. When your company goes into a crisis with the Gulf and the Deep Water Horizon spills, are you mentally prepared for the task, or will your response reflect poorly upon your character and your business? Unfortunately, Hayward was not up to the task.

We can try to sympathize a little bit with this CEO of a Fortune 100 company, as he probably did want "life to go on" for everyone who was hurt by the event. Unfortunately, his company was responsible for the worst oil spill in the history of mankind. It was a lack of mental preparation that opened the door for him to make a callous, uncaring, and self-centered statement. Hayward's behavior represents a good example of what happens when you are used to being on TV and trust your own impulses on auto-pilot, rather than preparing.

You might think, "Oh, I'm just going to go in front of CNN. Because I've talked to CNN plenty of times, I'm able to handle this pressure-filled situation." While I have no direct proof, I strongly suspect Hayward didn't invest enough time in mental preparation to make sure his comments would be diplomatic and well-received by an angry public.

BRINGING IN THE SUPPORT TEAM

One must allocate enough time to first mentally prepare for a goal or task. If there is still a strong sense of skepticism or self-doubt after preparing to the best of one's ability, then the support team should step in. For example, with future marathon prep, I plan to take into consideration how much I weigh, how much I train, and use those figures to calculate a realistic run time.

I will evaluate the potential effects of many more factors, and discuss those with people who support me and understand my individual needs. There is significance in the amount of information we gather to make a decision, and finding reliable sources of information is also important for a CEO. The amount of information, quality of information, and sources of information are all incredibly valuable when seeking to be as mentally prepared as possible.

If we mentally prepare in isolation, then we're limited to only having our own perspectives and all the "blind spots" that come with these. There's a logistical challenge in making sure you have enough time to engage the right people. Some situations might not require that much information, but many do. I frequently see CEOs under-prepare. They could have prepared differently had they taken initiative to involve others in their planning and decision-making.

BEST PRACTICES AROUND MENTAL PREPARATION

CEOs in larger organizations have an uncanny ability to focus on only a few things that are most important. They are able to set up their schedules in order to give enough time to those things. What are some best practices Endurance Executives are employing? I counsel my CEO clients on a number of tactics.

The first item is a concept called "quiet time." This period extends from when you wake up, until you start to think about work at the beginning of your day. It also is when you end the work day, until the time you go to sleep. Many CEOs go full-steam from sun up to sun down, which contributes to the feeling of being spread thin, and always tense. Creating quiet time at the beginning and end of the day will contribute greatly to keeping the tension, stress, and/or anxiety to manageable levels. An Endurance Executive uses his or her quiet time to exercise, rest, or spend valuable time with family or friends.

The second critical item is to organize your day so you have enough time at the beginning of the work day to organize your tasks, and identify the most important events and their desired outcomes. This way, you can mentally prepare for them. I see CEOs cut more corners here than anywhere else. This time allotment positions Endurance Executives for success, but lack of investment made here puts many a leader on thin ice.

The third item for an Endurance Executive to keep in mind is the need to break up their day, creating gaps to allow for de-escalating tension and preparing for the next important event of the day. As the day evolves, it is critical to have gaps over the course of the morning, middle part of the day, and the afternoon. This ensures there is a moment to focus on what is most important, and invest in last-minute preparations to ensure the best outcomes.

At end of the work day, it is important to take an inventory for the day, addressing personal performance, leadership, and overall team performance. This helps create a clear course of action and follow-up items for the next day. It is impossible for a CEO to continue their growth journey if they are not holding themselves to a high standard on a consistent basis.

ENDURANCE EXECUTIVE MENTAL PREPARATION BEST PRACTICES

	MENTAL PREP	KEY EVENTS/MEETING
1 Quiet Time	START OF THE DAY	
2 Differentiate organizing tasks and meetings versus mentally preparing for the execution of each	START OF WORK DAY	
	MID MORNING	KEY MEETING #1
3 Key breaks in the day to de-elevate tension and focus on next key event/meeting	LUNCHTIME	
	MID AFTERNOON	KEY MEETING #2 & #3
4 Reconcile the day and organize tomorrow. Are you reflecting on where you succeed and failed?	END OF WORK DAY	
1 Quiet Time	END OF THE DAY	

We've touched on many different instances throughout the day during which a CEO can take time to mentally prepare and maintain focus on his performance. I don't recommend that a CEO incorporate all of these suggestions immediately, although over time it is important to find the rhythm that works best for them. How time is broken up will depend upon how many breaks over the course of the day one needs to reflect on today and prepare for tomorrow.

People need to look critically at their schedules, workflow and habits, in order to evaluate where breaks and preparation time will fit in. Some might do more preparation at the start of the day. Some might do more at the end of the day. It varies from person to person, but it all goes back to planning enough time to mentally prepare for the important things.

REFLECTION AND CLOSING THE MENTAL PREPARATION LOOP

A key part of improving your mental preparation is to reflect at the end of each day and think about how you performed relative to your desired outcomes, and how well you prepared. This is an intuitive journey; people who want to grow will learn and improve as they go. Every CEO I interviewed for this book credited their process of reflection as being a major source of learning and personal development.

The biggest challenge CEOs face is that they don't make time to do this with the frequency they need to sustain success. Taking responsibility for one's own planning, as well as how that influences overall performance on any given day, serves to close what I refer to as the "mental preparation loop." This loop can sometimes be painful, because it forces us to accept when we get it wrong. Did Tony Heyward ever hold himself accountable for his comments during the BP Gulf Oil spill? If he is an Endurance Executive, he has learned from the experience and continues to hold himself accountable today.

CHAPTER 7 SUMMARY

Mental preparation describes when an Endurance Executive visualizes the desired outcome—as well as all of the *possible* outcomes—of an important future interaction. Mental preparation is not just about organizing an agenda for the meeting; it is also thinking about all of the participants and how they will behave in the meeting. It is important to consider their perspectives in addition to what happens if things don't go as planned.

HEALTHY SKEPTICISM

A healthy sense of skepticism is an important tool to carry in your mental preparation toolkit. We all love to think things will go as planned. The skepticism will help drive additional preparation to avoid getting surprised.

BRINGING IN THE SUPPORT TEAM

One must allocate enough time to first mentally prepare for a goal or task. If there is still a strong sense of skepticism or self-doubt after preparing to the best of one's ability, then an Endurance Executive relies on help from the support team. A support team member can serve as a good sounding board as well as validate assumptions or offer alternatives points of view that can help an Endurance Executive broaden their view of a situation.

BEST PRACTICES AROUND MENTAL PREPARATION

CEOs in larger organizations have an uncanny ability to focus on only a few things that are most important. They are able to set up their schedules in a way that gives enough time to those things.

An Endurance Executive also is adept in these four areas, in terms of their self-management:

* Quiet Time: This period is from when you wake up until you start to think about work at the beginning of the day. It also is the period from when you stop thinking about work until you go to sleep. Many CEOs and other leaders have no quiet time because they allow work to be in their thoughts on a perpetual basis.

* Planning Time: Endurance Executives are adept at investing time at the beginning of the day to focus on the highest value items on their agenda, as well as to delegate items so they avoid becoming overloaded.

* Breaking up the Day: With any growth situation, new things will always pop up. An Endurance Executive does a good job of breaking up the day and keeping gaps in their schedule to allow for de-escalation.

REFLECTION AND CLOSING THE MENTAL PREPARATION LOOP

A key factor in improving your mental preparation is to reflect at the end of each day—think about how you performed relative to your desired outcomes, and how well you prepared. This aspect of mental preparation is often absent, making it difficult for a CEO or other leader to improve upon their last performance since they didn't reflect on the mental preparation that led to the performance in question.

ENDURANCE EXECUTIVE MENTAL PREPARATION BEST PRACTICES

	MENTAL PREP	KEY EVENTS/MEETING

1 — Quiet Time

START OF THE DAY

2 — Differentiate organizing tasks and meetings versus mentally preparing for the execution of each

START OF WORK DAY

MID MORNING — KEY MEETING #1

3 — Key breaks in the day to de-elevate tension and focus on next key event/meeting

LUNCHTIME

MID AFTERNOON — KEY MEETING #2 & #3

4 — Reconcile the day and organize tomorrow. Are you reflecting on where you succeed and failed?

END OF WORK DAY

1 — Quiet Time

END OF THE DAY

REFLECTIONS:

1. How much quiet time do you have at the start of the day?
2. How much quiet time do you have at the end of the day?
3. How do you decrease or manage your tension and stress levels over the course of the day?
4. Do you mentally prepare for important meeting and events by visualizing desired outcome?
5. How frequently do you do contingency planning for your key meetings and events?

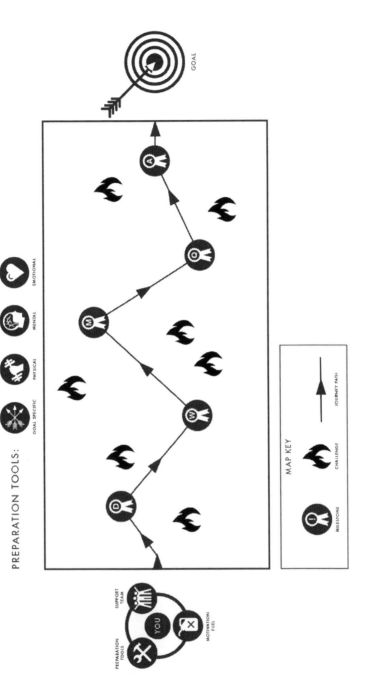

Chapter 8

EMOTIONAL PREPARATION

Sometimes a CEO's journey can be a lonely one, especially as they strive for growth and navigate into uncharted territories. In many cases, people never think about the preparation required for this undertaking. You don't *plan* on hitting the wall in the first place, so knowing how to be emotionally prepared for that impact isn't intuitive. You don't want to plan to fail. Lonely CEOs who are trying to grow their companies aren't planning to fail either. During that journey, we come across challenges—and we might hit the wall. We have to come to terms with that.

As with other aspects of preparation, a key part of ***mental preparation*** is reflecting on what has already taken place. I had a lot of time to reflect on what went wrong during the latter stages of my marathon. The last 5 miles were brutal, but at least I had Jen and Joe to get through the painful moments. In the later stages of the race, I thought about how I could have prepared emotionally for this point. We talked in an earlier chapter about how maintaining composure is the first step to recovery after hitting the wall. Once we have composed ourselves, we have to look inward.

Emotional preparation is the amount of time you spend looking inward and preparing for when things go wrong or off script. Mental preparation, on the other hand, is about visualizing the outcome. The moment you're in an unplanned situation, you find yourself in a space where you need both emotional control and mental agility. If your emotions take over, you will lose your mental agility, or the ability to think quickly on your feet.

Emotional preparation is asking oneself, "What if I face something unexpected? How will that make me feel?" According to the US Library of Medicine, an affiliate of the National Institute of Health, your brain processes logic 50 percent slower than your body processes emotional triggers. From a CEO's perspective, emotional preparation is important. Endurance Executives cannot afford to be impulsive; they need to be focused, attuned, and ready. The destructive tension that builds for a lot of CEOs is the result of an absence of emotional preparation, even lack of awareness of their own emotional states.

While it might sound like a revolutionary idea to some, emotion is always within your control. However, if you're not attuned to understanding where you are at the moment, what can happen is called, "the amygdala hijack." It's the fight-or-flight response that kicks in instantly. This term was coined by Daniel Goleman in his book, *Emotional Intelligence*. It occurs when a feeling of being threatened stimulates our more primitive brain functions toward fight or flight behavior. The amygdala hijack is an instinctual response that, in the business world, can cause leaders or employees to become defensive when their ideas are challenged. Some people lose their tempers and behave in ways that are inappropriate for the workplace when a sense of looming threat puts them into fighting mode.

If we want to be at our very best, we have to allocate time to physical training in addition to mental and emotional preparation. Together, all three help to reduce our stress levels. Reducing stress levels lower the likelihood of amygdala hijack, and embarrassing situations (or worse!). It can be a lot of work to control our emotions and be prepared, but doing the work, seeing that you ultimately decide how you feel, emote, and respond, will put you in control of every situation you're likely to face.

I want CEOs, and other leaders who read this book, to walk away with an understanding that they must invest more time into reflecting. Ideally, mental and emotional preparation should happen at the start of the day, and reflection should come in the middle or end of the day. It will be different for each individual, but the more we reflect, the more we learn about ourselves, our feelings, and why we feel the way we do.

The more we reflect and learn, the better position we are in to make the right decisions. We may choose to pursue an additional opportunity based on having an enthusiastic emotional state rather than considering, "I need to take it easy for a couple of months, because the chance of my success keeping this schedule is probably not so good."

We need to be honest with ourselves to be in tune with how we're doing physically and mentally. An individual suffering from mental fatigue can't necessarily visualize how they can contribute more energy to an additional project, or what that investment would require in the most practical sense. When you have emotional fatigue, you might not be in tune with how you're feeling. Becoming disconnected from your feelings increases your chances of falling short of your goals—or worse, hitting the wall.

It can get very lonely at the top for a CEO. Those who are not reflecting, and not talking about their emotions, will lack the emotional preparation needed to perform at their best level. When I reflect on my life as a CEO, I saw my greatest growth when I realized it was incredibly important for me to have different types of preparation. Becoming a business leader meant beginning a journey for which it was important to prepare physically, mentally, and emotionally.

The physical and mental preparation came to me easily, but emotional preparation took a while to perfect. My lack of experience as a

CEO during my 20s is partially what caused me to fall short on emotional preparation. Emotional development accompanies increased age, wisdom, and maturity levels, so it can take a lot longer to make progress on that front. I was able to catch up in this area when I invested more time in reflection. Time for reflection can benefit people of all ages, even those who have had three, four, or five decades to accumulate wisdom.

To some degree, making improvements in my own emotional preparation was accelerated by the introspection that came after my mom's passing. I had to rely on reflection even further when my wife and I faced challenges surrounding our son Jack's development, and the uncertainty that came with raising a special needs child.

I also leveraged my support teams to discuss the challenges I was having with emotional preparation. Examples of this included sharing with them what was I was most concerned about at particular times. Sometimes, it was a difficult customer, or a problem employee. Talking about the effect these scenarios had on me wasn't always easy, but it was part of learning how to manage similar situations for the future.

Endurance Executives are committed to success, and create circles of friends and colleagues with whom they can discuss their emotionally-driven concerns. It's important to spend time reflecting on these concerns outside of discussions with one's support team, in order to come up with a plan that will help you cope. Whether it's managing the stress around a new acquisition, or frustration about an employee's underperformance, personal reflection time— combined with the input of a strong support team—will help an Endurance Executive make wise, timely, and appropriate decisions.

There are plenty of CEOs who do invest time in reflection and emotional preparation. Strive to increase consistency in reflection and preparation, and the more successful and ambitious you become. We all meet people who can support us, so it's counterproductive to not use these people as resources. Friends, colleagues, and support team members want to help. They want to be an active part of your success.

Some CEOs are not prepared to let others in, and oftentimes they languish at a career plateau. They feel they lack answers, simply because they have not used their support teams and loved ones as resources for emotional preparation. Many of the CEOs I've had the pleasure of working with have found new ways of growing when they allowed people into their emotional lives. I was lucky enough that they allowed me to help them see this flaw in their behavior, so other people could help them grow, and gain wisdom.

LEARNING FROM ADVERSITY

When I was hitting the wall, I thought about my mom, who is no longer with us, during every single mile. Thinking about her struggle helped me through the worst of the pain. I thought about others like my grandparents, who are no longer among the living. These thoughts weren't meant to be morbid, but rather, they kept me focused during my marathon. I wanted to persevere for them. I had the opportunity to persevere, but doing it just for me wasn't enough. I also wanted to do it for my son and wife, who struggled through so many challenges.

Although it's a cliché, "what doesn't kill you makes you stronger" is true. The experiences I had, seeing my mom in her decline at the hospital and hospice, helped me get through many difficult times that came after. The difficult nature of an extreme event brings perspective about what is important and what is trivial. It also helps us learn to tolerate extreme circumstances. I didn't want to go through the pain of seeing loved ones die or hurt, but those experiences prepare you for withstanding pain in other parts of life. While I was in pain trying to finish a marathon, it helped put things into perspective. My suffering would only be temporary compared to those loved ones who suffered and were no longer living.

THE MECHANICS OF EMOTIONAL PREPARATION

Emotional preparation and building self-awareness will help a CEO or Endurance Executive recognize and face the walls that appear over the course of a lifetime. Unfortunately, I didn't know what the wall looked like before my race, and by the time I realized, it was too late. Now that I am familiar with weaknesses in my physical, mental, and emotional preparation, I think it's incredibly important that I be on the lookout for the warning signs.

The same applies to the work and lives of CEOs. They need to look out for warning signs indicating potential hazards for which they should prepare. When there's a high-stakes deal, a major acquisition or sale to make, they want to be at their best. If they're committed to success, it's imperative to revisit how they've been preparing emotionally for their success.

We are going to build on the framework for mental preparation.

BALANCING MENTAL & EMOTIONAL PREPARATION

	MENTAL PREP	KEY EVENTS/MEETING
1 — Quiet Time	START OF THE DAY	
2 — Differentiate organizing tasks and meetings versus mentally preparing for the execution of each	START OF WORK DAY	Add time for emotional preparation
	MID MORNING	KEY MEETING #1
3 — Key breaks in the day to de-elevate tension and focus on next key event/meeting	LUNCHTIME	What is your emotional temperature at each point and how do you adapt?
	MID AFTERNOON	KEY MEETING #2 & #3
4 — Reconcile the day and organize tomorrow. Are you reflecting on where you succeed and failed?	END OF WORK DAY	How did you feel during your key meetings and how well did you manage your emotions?
1 — Quiet Time	END OF THE DAY	

LOOKING BACKWARDS HELPS US SEE THE FUTURE

In the last chapter, we talked about breaking up the day so we can spend time focusing on what might happen later. A key part of emotional preparation is looking backwards, while mental preparation is about preparing to move forward. Mental preparation is about visualizing a goal and thinking about what comes next as you prepare to fulfill that goal. Emotional preparation, to a great degree, involves reviewing what's already transpired. Emotional maturity is recognizing and taking ownership for both your actions and responses to specific events when they occur.

* How did the outcome make you feel?
* As you review the experience, what emotions lead up to the final decision?
* Were you happy with how you performed?
* Were you able to stay calm?
* Did you keep fear out of the equation?
* During a slow or complicated negotiation, were you able to avoid feelings of anger or irritation?

REFLECTION AND HONESTY

Honesty can be a synonym for authenticity. People can't forget who they are, so when they lie to themselves and rationalize certain actions or feelings, it can lead to a downward spiral. At the very least, it keeps them stuck on a plateau, unable to improve, or continue to grow past a certain point.

Sometimes, if we don't have enough time to prepare by engaging others, then reflecting on your own choices and behaviors in isolation is better than nothing. For example, busy people can go through periods where they have important, back-to-back meetings on consecutive days.

They are crunched for time already. Between commutes and participation in so many meetings, logistically, they don't have a moment to engage others during a time when feedback would be most helpful.

In an ideal world, we would all have time to reflect on our concerns with others, and get feedback even at the busiest of times. Occasionally, it may be worthwhile to consider if meetings can be postponed, or your schedule rearranged in such a way that you will have an extra hour.

Use this time to consult with your support team about important, pressing issues. External feedback from your support team can validate whether or not you're being honest with yourself regarding how you've assessed the dynamics of a situation, your plan for action, and your overall feelings.

In preparation for my race, I thought I engaged enough people and gathered enough feedback to improve my likelihood of hitting my four-hour goal. It turned out that I came up a little short. I hadn't lost the 10 extra pounds I needed to lose, which would have increased my chances of running the ideal time.

Even if I'd lost the weight, and maintained a flawless training regimen, this being my first marathon, I would have been well advised to have found a more experienced runner. This person might have said to me, "Alex, you train other people to not be overly ambitious, so let's be honest with yourself." In reflection, I realized poignantly that what was missing in my equation was honesty with myself. I should have thought, "I'm going to try my best, and know that every step forward is a small victory, regardless of my finishing time."

Just running a marathon is an accomplishment, a reason to feel proud, and each time a runner completes a race, he or she learns more skills to apply to future races. An athlete's first marathon should be about self-honesty, and starting a journey that extends far beyond the finish line.

CONNECTING WITH YOUR EMOTIONAL INTELLIGENCE

When addressing issues of performance, I reference **emotional intelligence**, and the work of Daniel Goleman, a leading expert in the field. Goleman's work broke down emotional intelligence into five areas: motivation, self-awareness, self-regulation, empathy, and social skills.

In Chapter 2, we talked about motivation and its three components—passion, desire, and commitment. In other chapters, we've talked about self-awareness through reflection. Something we haven't talked about, but alluded to, is self-regulation.

In Goleman's book, *The Emotionally Intelligent Workplace*, he talks about the Emotional Intelligence Competency Inventory he helped developed in 2000, with the assistance of two other influential PhDs of his time, Dr. Richard Boyatzis and Dr. Kenneth Rhee. Self-regulation is broken down into trust, adaptability, conscientiousness, and discipline.

An Endurance Executive has to be conscientious and have a great degree of discipline to pursue all of their ambitious goals. Trust plays an enormous role. One must trust his or her support team and other people, to be able to use their help to succeed. The alternative to developing trust with others is the "lonely road" we referred to frequently in this chapter.

Lastly, an Endurance Executive has to be adaptable. They risk falling short of their goals if they are too rigid. The business landscape has changed dramatically since the economic recession of 2008 and 2009. This highlights the need for Endurance Executives to be able to adapt to a changing landscape. Adaptability is a character trait that enables leaders to persevere though the wall.

I was fortunate to be a person who, despite hitting the wall, was prepared to modify my plans so I could finish the race, no matter what. I knew I had to be ready for the wall, though I'd planned for it to come much later in the race.

A CEO or ambitious high-level executive is always refining his or her ability to adapt. Otherwise, when they are forced to adapt to a situation, the absence of practice will show in the low rate of adaptation to the new situation. That can be critical when the economy is failing, or competition is escalating.

DISCIPLINE

Discipline is a trait often misunderstood, and in many cases, people assume they have more self-discipline than they actually do. Levels of discipline vary for every person. People often mistake ambitious CEOs as having a great degree of discipline. They may have a decent amount of discipline, but discipline is like a glass of water (and this is where we go back to the mentality of conservation versus consumption): If you're not careful with that glass of discipline, you might expend it on areas where you won't get a good return on your effort.

Not getting a good return on your discipline would be similar to spilling your water. If you're mindful of using your discipline when you need it the most, you will get great use out of this resource.

In other cases, some ambitious CEOs drink their whole glass of discipline at work, and their personal or family goals suffer when the discipline is no longer available to pursue needs outside of work. An Endurance Executive conserves discipline to drink enough for work, while saving some for personal and family pursuits as well.

There's a close correlation between energy and discipline. There's also a correlation between your personal energy level and how fast your discipline will be replenished. If you have low energy, it takes a long time to replenish your discipline. If you have high energy, and much enthusiasm to apply to important tasks, you quickly replenish your discipline.

Successful preparation happens when you are taking care of yourself through physical preparation like exercise, relaxation, and quality time with friends and family. If we are not taking care of ourselves and are working too many hours for an extended period of time, our discipline will suffer due to low energy and low rate of discipline regeneration. This is the correlation between physical preparation and emotional preparation. Both directly affect our energy levels.

EMPATHY AND SOCIAL SKILLS

The issue of empathy is something that one might not think of as important in sports. Empathy is your ability to understand how someone else is feeling. It is critical that your support team has empathy, and it's hypocritical for you to expect people to be empathetic with you when you're not empathetic with them. You must have empathy, in turn, for your support team.

It's important for an endurance CEO, or any leader, to collaborate with people and have great discussions. You need to develop your empathy so you're in the right frame of mind to engage in productive collaborative efforts, and to understand the needs of those you support and lead.

The final component of emotional intelligence is one's grasp of social skills. Having good social skills means finding positive, constructive ways to interact with other people. As a leader becomes better at developing relationships, and developing the skill sets of his or her subordinates, the symbiotic relationship between a CEO and his or her support team grows stronger and stronger. You might have heard the adage, "Great leaders also make great followers." This is a fact.

The more ambitious we are, the more we must invest mentally and emotionally in the preparation that will enable us to stay in control of our emotions. We can accomplish that goal by investing time into thinking about how we might feel if things don't go as planned, and come up with some tactics to help us cope when plans go awry. Additionally, emotional preparation involves reflecting on what took place, how events unfolded, and the emotions we associate with these events. The CEOs I see, who have been successful for long periods of time, have done a good job investing time into their own individual emotional preparation, have the right support teams around them, and have used their wisdom and informed perspectives to help mentor others.

CHAPTER 8 SUMMARY

This type of preparation is about reflecting on one's feeling leading up to, during, and after an important interaction. Many CEOs and other leaders don't spend enough time thinking about how they felt before, during, and after a situation until experiencing enough bad outcomes motivates them to reassess this aspect of their performance.

LEARNING FROM ADVERSITY

Adversity and negative experiences assist us in our commitment to avoid a similar bad experience. When we reflect on adversity, it is important to draw key learning lessons from these situations, especially in how an Endurance Executive was able to persevere through it.

THE MECHANICS OF EMOTIONAL PREPARATION

Emotional preparation happens when we reflect. It might happen at the end of the day when we reflect upon the day that just took place, or it could occur in the middle of the day if an Endurance Executive has a time gap to reflect on negative feelings and adjust them accordingly.

Lastly, we can improve our emotional preparation by reflecting at the beginning of the day. The prior is about what could happen and alternatives. Emotional preparation is reflecting on how your day might go, and how you might feel if things don't go as planned, especially if conflicts arise from other parties' lack of cooperation.

LOOKING BACKWARDS HELPS US SEE THE FUTURE

A key component of emotional preparation is the ability to look backwards. An Endurance Executive must be able to scrutinize how they felt during the most important moments of their day. I have seen firsthand how this type of reflection drives better decision-making and helps CEOs and other leaders develop their leadership skills

REFLECTION AND HONESTY

Honesty can be a synonym for authenticity, so people can't forget who they are. If CEOs or executives lie to themselves about a bad performance and rationalize certain actions or feelings, it can lead to negative outcomes. Ignoring these problems can create a blind spot—or worse—lead to a downward spiral in the CEO's abilities because they are not owning up to a bad performance.

CONNECTING WITH YOUR EMOTIONAL INTELLIGENCE

When addressing issues of performance, I reference "emotional intelligence," and the work of Daniel Goleman, a leading expert in the field. Goleman's work broke down emotional intelligence into five areas: motivation, self-awareness, self-regulation, empathy, and social skills.

DISCIPLINE

Discipline is a trait often misunderstood, and in many cases, people assume they have more self-discipline than they actually do. Treat discipline as a scarce resource and deploy it in the highest value areas.

EMPATHY AND SOCIAL SKILLS

There are two key areas of emotional intelligence that are important to highlight. An Endurance Executive will leverage empathy to ensure that they understand how someone else is feeling—especially when a difficult conversation or high-stakes meeting is coming up. The second area of emotional intelligence, social skills, involves an Endurance Executive's ability to develop relationships. I have worked with many CEOs and other leaders who hit a plateau because they were unable to develop deep relationships with the people they relied upon to help their respective companies. The root cause of the skill gap is not investing enough time to develop social skills.

BALANCING MENTAL & EMOTIONAL PREPARATION

	MENTAL PREP	KEY EVENTS/MEETING

1 — Quiet Time — START OF THE DAY

2 — Differentiate organizing tasks and meetings versus mentally preparing for the execution of each — START OF WORK DAY — Add time for emotional preparation

MID MORNING — KEY MEETING #1

3 — Key breaks in the day to de-elevate tension and focus on next key event/meeting — LUNCHTIME — What is your emotional temperature at each point and how do you adapt?

MID AFTERNOON — KEY MEETING #2 & #3

4 — Reconcile the day and organize tomorrow. Are you reflecting on where you succeed and failed? — END OF WORK DAY — How did you feel during your key meetings and how well did you manage your emotions?

1 — Quiet Time — END OF THE DAY

REFLECTIONS

1. How frequently do we reflect about our emotions?
2. Have you engaged with members of your support team in discussing some of your challenges around different aspects of emotional intelligence: Self Awareness, Self Regulation, Motivation, Empathy and Social Skills?

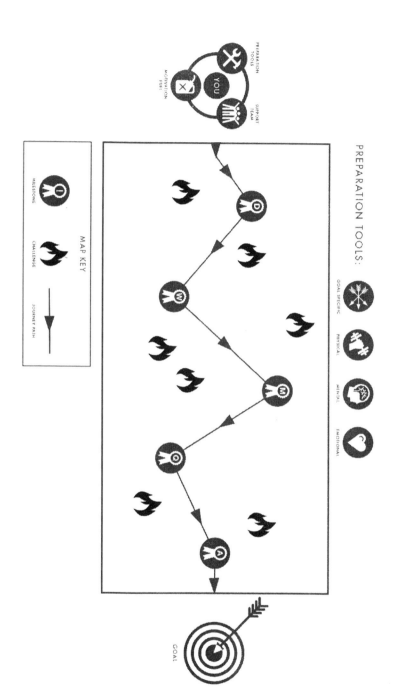

JOURNEY MAP:

PREPARATION TOOLS:

GOAL SPECIFIC

PHYSICAL

MENTAL

EMOTIONAL

YOU

PREPARATION TOOLS

MOTIVATION FUEL

SUPPORT TEAM

MAP KEY

MILESTONE

CHALLENGE

JOURNEY PATH

GOAL

Chapter 9

•　•　•

PHYSICAL PREPARATION

P hysical fitns health through exercise is actually a process based on learning your needs and how to best accommodate those needs. With all of the different priorities in people's lives, the challenge lies in making time to take care of yourself physically, including working out. It's important to understand, especially for hard-charging CEOs, that your body is your motor. If you want it to run smoothly, you have to take care of it.

How committed are you to your success? Commitment to executive success, at a minimum, requires putting forth effort to take care of the physical body. An unhealthy body will create inherent challenges for any c-level executive. My experience with work-oriented, driven Endurance CEOs is that they do take care of their fitness. They do some form of exercise as a release for stress, and to help them feel good about themselves.

While an individual will make progress from doing "cardio," there is more to what is occurring inside our bodies than just the obvious. "Cardiovascular exercise, especially for males, stimulates the release of testosterone and fires endorphins into the body. This biochemical response also happens during times of daily life stress, or high pressure at work or home, and can fuel impulsive behaviors in inappropriate environments.

The key is to channel that stress, vulnerability and impulsive behavior into exercise, or it may come out in less constructive ways.

In my work during the last five years, coaching ambitious CEOs and high level executives, I noticed that some have a tendency to exercise too much. The exercise helps these people stay in great physical shape, but their stress levels remain high, as do instances of non-productive impulsive behavior. Seeing this seemingly counterintuitive behavior led me to examine how these executives were balancing exercise with rest and relaxation.

I found some interesting patterns. For example, those who exercise intensely and frequently, while also getting adequate rest and relaxation to facilitate healthy recovery will see increases in overall energy levels and mental well-being. Those who continue to work out with intense focus and devotion, but are unable to devote adequate time to recovery will see the benefits of exercise plateau quickly. The physical trauma caused by challenging workouts, day after day, without enough rest afterwards, results in over-trained, exhausted bodies and minds that do not perform well physically, mentally or emotionally. During periods of over-training, the resting heart rate may be elevated. Endurance Executives may also feel increased sensitivity to stress triggers, or even a sense of feeling too "tightly wound."

Just getting in shape isn't enough if we want to continue to grow and experience sustained high levels of performance in all aspects of our lives. From a conservation perspective, a lot of CEOs don't spend time allowing their bodies to rest and relax when they are not exercising. Training for a marathon taught me the value of rest and regeneration. While training as intensely as I did, I had to rest my legs or otherwise, I was going to struggle out there. I adopted a program that was on the aggressive side in terms of total miles per week. It was possible that I over-trained, because I didn't find the perfect balance between exercise, rest and regeneration for my first marathon.

REST AND RELAXATION

While it may seem counterintuitive to many CEOs and leaders, rest, relaxation and regeneration is important when it comes to physical preparation. People will change their daily behavior from hour to hour if their iPhone is low on battery. If it's only halfway through a workday, and an individual knows he or she has an important business call they must make on their cell phone later that afternoon, they simply stop sending out unnecessary texts or Tweeting, to prioritize conservation and save resources for the more important priority. Yet, these same people won't change their behavior if their body is feeling run-down.

Think of your body as your mobile device, and your level of exhaustion as the remaining battery power. Do you need to slow down the amount of information you're sending out today in order to perform your best later?

If you are wondering how you can find ways to relax and regenerate, there are many ways you can achieve this. Get a massage; sit back and read something you enjoy, or just reflect on the day, as long as your body is resting. Some of the best advice I ever got was from the commencement speaker during my graduation from undergraduate business school, whose name I've long since forgotten.

She said, "You have to learn how to do nothing." The guidance didn't really make sense to me at the time. It struck me as an absurd statement when I was graduating college. I need to learn to do nothing? Like many college-aged people, I'd already spent many hours wasting time. What I learned later in life, and try to counsel other CEOs, is that your body needs to disconnect. Your body needs outlets for recovery, as well as for physical fitness. Relaxation is an important aspect of physical preparation because it reduces stress, tension, anxiety and the probability of impulsive behavior.

Kim Nelson, our dynamic CEO and tri-athlete from Toronto, is adamant about and sensitive to her needs to rest her body as she has aged. Because of the extreme nature of a triathlon, rest becomes all the more important. Kim has 3 different coaches, one for each triathlon discipline, who hold her accountable for setting aside appropriate amounts of recovery time! Cal Ripken also changed his off-season workout habits as he grew older. He knew he had to adjust in order to be at peak performance and it only got harder as he grew older. The same applies in the work world, so we cannot take it lightly. Who is holding you accountable to rest your body so you can be at peak performance?

LAUGHTER IS THE BEST MEDICINE

Another important aspect of physical preparation is the role of humor and laughter. More and more is being written about the medicinal and psychological benefit of laughter, and we continue to discover more amazing benefits. Laughter relieves stress and dissolves tension. Dan Pink, in his book *A Whole New Mind*, talks about laughter, sense of play and the impact of these important behaviors on people and teams.

Perhaps executives should become more methodical about incorporating laughter into how they prepare for their meetings with individuals and teams? What role can laughter play to help a team grow closer, improve productivity and become better overall? In my own experience, when I know I will go through a high workload month, I need to find a good comedy series to follow with my family so I can get my laughs. Last year, the most reliable series to provide relief was *The Office*. Where would I be without the team at Dunder Mifflin!

The last key to rest and regeneration is human interaction. Regardless of whether you're an introvert or an extrovert, human interaction, especially with loved ones, creates a sense of relaxation and regeneration that we all need. Being in the moment with this group of people allows you to detach from the factors in your life that create tension and stress. Leaders, especially CEOs, refuel on the great positive energy that comes from interacting with their friends, family and loved ones. They can let their guards down, as they don't have to be a CEO with these people. It can often take time for high level executives to learn to effectively transition from work mode to family mode.

The more we practice at making this transition, the easier the transition will become. A primary challenge of switching into family mode is dealing with the unique pressures that come along with filling whatever roles you take on in the context of your family life. It's not always easy to be a parent, spouse, sibling, or caregiver to aging family members. Transitioning from one role to another carries its own set of responsibilities and emotional maturity.

How individuals behave in their family lives, compared to their work lives, varies from person to person, but this too can be managed well, especially with time and practice. Ultimately, family mode should carry less pressure, and serve as a valuable vacation from the daily grind of an ambitious leader. The energy and relaxation derived from this type of quality human interaction helps an Endurance Executive reduce tension/stress, anxiety and to get focused on their goals.

Mental preparation also develops and matures when we participate in activities that promote reduction of stress and tension. Stress is a big distraction for someone who is visualizing a desired goal outcome, or exploring potential scenarios that might play out at work or at home. Reduced anxiety also helps the process of reflection, as it allows us to approach critical thought with a clear head and focused energy. Anxiety can make it difficult to connect with your other feelings when reflecting back on a situation and the associated emotions that were present throughout the experience.

MEASURING WORK + LIFE

Physical preparation requires planning methodically to reduce your stress, anxiety and tension. I believe in measuring things, in breaking challenges down into components and checklists so they become quantifiable units or values. In the case of stress, anxiety or tension, assessing a measurement is difficult. As an alternative approach, I challenge the CEOs I coach to pay closer attention to how they spend their time outside of work. I want them to be aware the work plus life equation also easily translates to physical preparation. This variation of the equation is as expressed as: $A + B + C =/> 12$ hours. Add up the hours you spend in a week with

* A = Exercise
* B = Relaxation(see examples from above)
* C = Quality time with friends and family

Do they add up to 12 or more hours a week? How did I come up with twelve? Well, I started paying attention to all of the people I coached over a period of two years, and considered the amount these people exercised. Three or four hours per week is a good amount to devote to exercise. Some of my more elite CEOs fancy themselves quite the athletes, and they'll get five hours or more. It's important to balance the amount of exercise with relaxation, and then to balance both of these variables with human interaction. Not just any human interaction, but quality interaction, such as sharing meals with loved ones, and going on excursions with family and friends. These exchanges lead to a variety of different positive emotional stimulus.

In our chapter on goal specific-preparation, we talked about the importance of always working on development of communication skills. As leaders, these skills help us get the most from our support groups. They also assist with building relationships during quality time spent with friends and family. Strong communication skills allow us to engage in a more substantive way, through listening and talking about things that matter to you and your loved ones.

As we've already learned, some people have quality interaction in their lives, along with adequate exercise, but the relaxation piece is a missing factor. Earlier in the chapter, I mentioned how I started seeing a pattern that if people weren't balancing exercise and rest and relaxation with quality time, then imbalances emerge. I created a second equation to depict what this looks like in a practical, applicable form: A + B = /< Quality time.

Values carry the same meaning and significance as in the previous equation, but the purpose of this variation is to ensure there is greater awareness between personal time and quality time with friends and family. The latter needs to get the most amount of time, followed by exercise and relaxation. When my clients focus on this equation, they see an immediate positive effect for two reasons. The obvious one is they make more time available for family and friends. The less obvious one is they start incorporating different forms of relaxation to help them disconnect from work.

PRIORITIZING: QUALITY TIME TAKES THE TOP SPOT

A lot of times, the CEOs who struggle most are those with competing demands for their time. If they prioritize those competing demands, first and foremost should be quality interaction with friends, family, and loved ones. Exercising, resting and relaxing should hold a lesser (but still extremely important) rank. In a perfect world, the numbers are seven hours or more of quality time with friends, family and loved ones per week.

Rest plus relaxation equals six or seven hours as well. Individuals who have great work+life equations will come closer to matching those ideal numbers. My CEO clients inevitably ask, "Where did these numbers come from?" I set the goal for quality time with friends and family at seven hours, because everyone I mentor has always thought one hour each day is a reasonable goal. When you miss that time because of working late or a business trip, you must ensure that you make up the time later.

The more an individual fixates on only success at work, the more they suffer from missing out on the happiness that comes from personal relationships. Like all relationships, our connections with spouses and loved ones must be nurtured through the investment of time and energy. Many people face challenges regarding intimacy. For example, it isn't always easy to talk about sensitive subjects with our friends and family. The less time you spend in interaction, the harder it is to have these types of conversations. If you're not investing enough time and energy into building intimacy, your relationships will fail.

Many CEOs struggle with this, and it is likely to become an underlying life issue, especially when a CEO has a young family. Having a lot of children can make one's work plus life balance extremely difficult to maintain at a healthy ratio, regardless of the amount of time you invest in developing intimacy. This potential pitfall can be a source of unhappiness, even for a CEO who seems to have it all.

In addition to one's family, spouse, and children, relationships with colleagues are also important. Much of a CEO's identity as an individual is wrapped up in their work persona or ego. A lot of their satisfaction is derived from gaining respect at work, as well as reciprocating that respect. When you lack interaction with others you respect, you will struggle to find validation.

This influences the mental and emotional well-being of those who have built a life and career around leadership. When you get validation, you feel as if you're being supported. This carries the physical benefit of stress relief in addition to the more obvious mental and emotional outcomes. Less stress manifests physically as healthier blood pressure, greater ability to invest time into exercise, and less likelihood of turning to alcohol or food as a source of comfort.

STRESS

Even though it may seem like a no-brainer, people continue to disregard the impact of stress. We talked about stress a little bit in the context of distractions. When we're pursuing goals, stress is a distracter that gets in the way. Preparation to manage stress must happen on three fronts: physically, mentally, and emotionally. Just understanding what you need to do physically will help you deescalate stress. I recognize when stress is affecting me physically, as I start to feel tension in my neck, shoulders and lower back. You need to understand what your own physical triggers and symptoms feel like.

For me, there are very few things that diminish stress faster than taking a run outside. Outdoors activities are relaxing for many people. If you are interested in running, hiking or participating in sports, keep in mind that there is extreme heat and cold in many climates. These extremes have a way of limiting our enjoyment of the outdoors, so we must stay in tune with physical demands, limitations and respond accordingly.

On certain days, a run outdoors may not be possible for you, so it is important to find a different activity that will help you diminish stress. Many people I have coached have one go-to exercise, but no alternatives for times when weather or immediate circumstances are not conducive to that particular type of workout. Knowing this about yourself and having alternatives to help you manage your stress is a big part of being an Endurance Executive.

Every person, regardless of their job or position in life, carries a need for physical preparation and for a general awareness of when they have pushed their body to the limit. We have to understand and be realistic at what we can expect from your bodies. If you're committed to achieving success, there are only so many 60, 80 or 90-hour work weeks you can pull, one after another, before suffering total exhaustion.

As we get older, our increasing physical limitations remind us regularly of our age, and that keeps us from logging the hours we did in our 20s and 30s. I'm 43 now, and I'm not ashamed to say that I can't work as many hours as I used to. As mentioned in a previous chapter, this is why we work smarter, not harder. This wisdom also extends to the physical realm.

When I say "sprint," I mean running fast. In any race, there are times you will sprint, as opposed to maintaining a slower-paced marathon mindset. When you sprint in an endurance race, you make sacrifices to your energy stores, stress your body and resources. I unfortunately ran too fast over the first 13 miles of my marathon, and much to my chagrin, I paid for it dearly.

When we think about sacrifices, especially in a marathon or endurance situation, you always have to prepare your body ahead of time for the possibility of needing to utilize your resources. I'm not advocating for people to work 80 to 90 hours each week, but if you're an ambitious CEO going after a big deal or major acquisition, you position yourself for greater success if you have physically prepared your body for that type of increased workload. Where you would normally put 60 hours into your workweek, you might find yourself investing in a two, four, or eight-week sprint of working 80-90 hours. This type of sprinting is like working at 125% of what you would normally perform.

Over an extended period of time, this incredible effort wears on the body and mind, but I've seen many successful CEOs who know how to identify when they can jog, and when they need to sprint. If you want to grow as an endurance leader, your body has to be prepared for any challenge the future might bring. It is necessary to stay in tune with where you stand in regards to your weekly exercise, rest and relaxation, and most importantly, the quality time that you derive from your relationships.

CHAPTER 9 SUMMARY

Physical fitness is not intuitive. Improving one's health through exercise is actually a process based on learning your needs and figuring out how to best accommodate those needs.

REST AND RELAXATION

Rest, relaxation, and regeneration are important when it comes to taking care of your body. If you don't take care of your body, your performance as a CEO or other leader will suffer over time.

LAUGHTER IS THE BEST MEDICINE

A valuable tool for physical preparation is humor and laughter. The positive emotions that come out of these two elements help reduce stress and tension. They also help create positive energy to tackle difficult tasks or situation.

MEASURING WORK + LIFE

Physical preparation requires planning methodically to reduce your stress, anxiety, and tension. I believe in measuring things, in breaking challenges down into components and checklists so they become quantifiable units or values. Track how you spend your time in these areas:

* A = Exercise
* B = Relaxation (rest, laughter, humor, etc)
* C = Quality time with friends and family

Rule 1: Work + Life Target: A + B + C > 12 hours

If an Endurance Executive is successful with Rule 1, then Rule 2 can be considered to continue elevating their success.

Rule 2: Work + Life Target: A + B < C

PRIORITIZING: QUALITY TIME TAKES THE TOP SPOT
A common challenge for CEOs and other leaders is competing demands for their time. If they prioritize those competing demands, first and foremost should be quality interaction with friends, family, and loved ones. The positive energy from this quality time is indisputable. The negative energy that arises when you neglect this area is extremely disruptive.

STRESS
We talked about the impact of stress earlier in the book. An Endurance Executive knows that physical preparation is the easiest way to manage it. Growth and ambition can cause a CEO or other leader to work long hours (aka sprint). An Endurance Executive is mindful of this and avoids "sprinting" for an extended period of time due to the potential risks.

REFLECTIONS:

1. How well do you do in rest and relaxation?
2. Have you leveraged the power of humor to help you manage stress?
3. Is your work+life physical preparation equation (A + B + C > 12)
4. Is your quality time with friends and family (C) greater than the sum of your exercise and rest and relaxation?

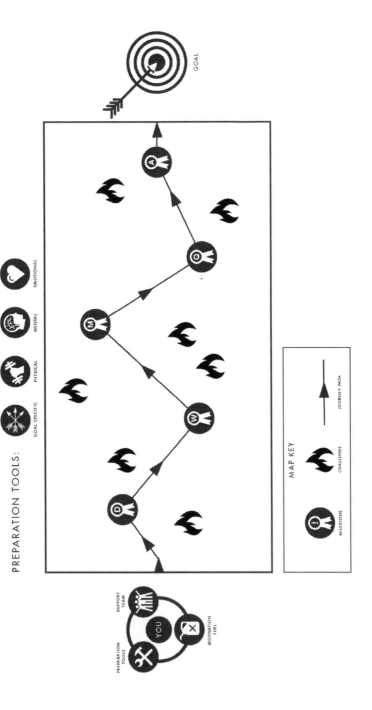

JOURNEY MAP:

PREPARATION TOOLS:

GOAL SPECIFIC

PHYSICAL

MENTAL

EMOTIONAL

GOAL

PREPARATION TOOLS

SUPPORT TEAM

YOU

MOTIVATION FUEL

MAP KEY

MILESTONE

CHALLENGE

JOURNEY PATH

Chapter 10

ENDURANCE LEADERSHIP & COACHING

When we seek to help others learn and grow, we also grow and mature emotionally. The insights we share with others also help us to see important aspects of our own personalities, strengths and weaknesses. Our communication skills improve as we learn how to provide constructive guidance, and our abilities to build positive relationships are also expanded.

In order to nurture the Endurance Executive mindset, even CEOs need to be good coaches, so they can always be learning about themselves through supporting others. I have developed a coaching methodology based on what I have learned as a CEO, and from studying the habits of other CEOs I admire.

We will talk about some basic things that can help people grow into great coaches These include how to prepare for and execute a great coaching session, how to conduct a coaching debrief, and the pitfalls associated with coaching.

All great coaching starts with preparation. Many times, executives make the mistake of trying to coach on an ad hoc, on-demand basis. I half jokingly refer to this as, "drive by coaching." Drive-by coaching is when you find yourself on the receiving end of a critique, at a time when you weren't expecting it. Many CEOs impulsively react with ad hoc coaching when they hear or see a problem.

The main flaw with this method is that they respond too quickly, not realizing that the person they are coaching mostly needed to be heard, or to vent. Because we desire to help them, we can feel compelled to coach them, but sometimes just lending an ear is what is most needed. One of the more important pieces of wisdom that CEOs can take away from this is to be mindful when someone needs help. Do they need someone to listen to them, or do they need someone to coach them?

They may also need coaching, but if you want to be effective, you need to prepare for giving constructive feedback and make sure the participant is willing to be coached. Here is a diagram of what that cycle looks like.

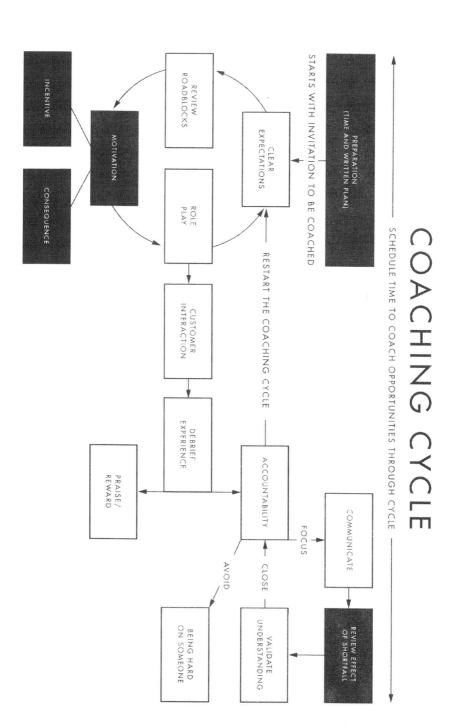

COACHING CYCLE

SCHEDULE TIME TO COACH OPPORTUNITIES THROUGH CYCLE

STARTS WITH INVITATION TO BE COACHED

PREPARATION
(TIME AND WRITTEN PLAN)

CLEAR EXPECTATIONS

REVIEW ROADBLOCKS

ROLE PLAY

MOTIVATION

INCENTIVE

CONSEQUENCE

CUSTOMER INTERACTION

RESTART THE COACHING CYCLE

DEBRIEF EXPERIENCE

PRAISE/ REWARD

ACCOUNTABILITY

FOCUS

COMMUNICATE

AVOID

CLOSE

BEING HARD ON SOMEONE

VALIDATE UNDERSTANDING

REVIEW EFFECT OF SHORTFALL

Following through with a fully developed coaching cycle means planning your upcoming interaction with the individual seeking feedback. It's hard to help someone if they're not a consenting adult. Regardless of whether it's in a classroom or a professional situation, individuals on the receiving end must have the desire to receive feedback. Talking at someone who doesn't want to hear your suggestions is called delivering a monologue, not coaching.

For someone to be an impactful coach, they need to invite others to participate mindfully and interactively in the session. Even those who've agreed to be a part of a coaching session may need to feel a sense of connection with their coach in order to fully engage and participate mentally. The way you choose to invite them into the scenario and your general tactfulness, will influence how quickly they connect, and how much they care about the session.

Here are some tactful ways to invite participation in a coaching session:

* "Is this a good time?"
* "Are you ready to review some possible goals for improvement?"
* "Are you ready to hear feedback that might make you uncomfortable?"

Many times we don't give those around us the courtesy of inviting them into conversations. These conversations can be extremely important and the invitation sets the tone for a meaningful exchange. The invitation style becomes even more important when an extroverted leader is coaching an introverted direct report. The invitation's delivery should be done in a slow and methodical way so it doesn't seem threatening. Part of planning a successful coaching session is being clear about the topics you will be addressing. Is your session focused on how to manage time better, or a conceptual issue like how become less impulsive?

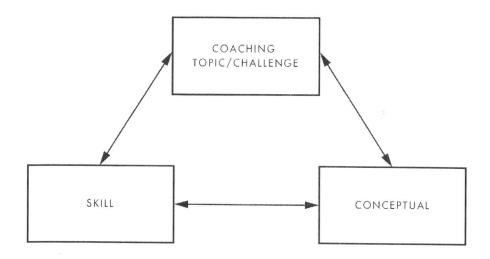

Having a clear topic to coach increases the chances of having successful session. There are coaching challenges that must be addressed from both a skill perspective and a conceptual perspective. An example of this is when a CEO coaches a direct report about how to hold someone accountable. The tactics used to hold people accountable make up the skill components of teaching and practicing accountability.

The conceptual challenge of accountability for some people can be centered around their own insecurities about managing difficult situations. If you as a coach try to address multiple challenges in a single session, it will most likely not be successful. Be patient when coaching people through complex scenarios because it can take many sessions to get through one complicated challenge.

·It's incredibly important when coaching, to review all of the road blocks. During the marathon, I needed someone to coach me on keeping a close eye on my heart rate. I needed guidance from an experienced pro, who could tell me to be careful going uphill, and at a certain pace at each mile mark. I take full responsibility for the pace I went out at.

In a coaching situation, it's important to be aware of all the road blocks, risks and dangers, so one can be fully accountable when it's time to manage these risks and dangers. Reviewing potential road blocks helps eliminate possible excuses.

If you're coaching about an issue that has become widespread or chronic, you have to consider the subject's source of motivation. This will help them have a better understanding of the problem, and desire to make positive changes. On more than one occasion over past couple of years, I have coached senior leaders who struggled with holding people accountable.

When I coached on accountability, I always asked people what motivated them and their teams. Leaders must identify the scenarios in which they are most motivated to address accountability issues, as well as how to prioritize these. For example, are you motivated enough to hold someone else accountable in a conflict management situation?

A lot of people feel they don't need to learn anymore. They don't have the motivation to learn, to be the best, or to be elite. That attitude makes it hard to continue to grow. As a coach, you must find a way to motivate individuals to make positive changes, and what motivates you to encourage behavior change in others. In the cases I mentioned, many leaders eventually made progress, after I held them accountable.

I was able to get them connected to the positive feelings they associated with being motivated to help their teams. It took a while to get them to see the opportunity as a way of helping others, versus disciplining them. Keep in mind that, as the session approaches its conclusion, you must confirm their understanding of what has been discussed, to ensure the motivation approach has resonated with them.

When I am actively coaching a CEO about having conversations with their workers, I want to hear what the proposed conversation will sound like—especially if it will be an interaction with someone they might have previously been too easy, or too tough, on. When I hear what they are going to say, I have proof, that they will be successful.

It's not good enough for them to tell me they're going to engage in a coaching session. It's not enough for them to tell me they understand. I need to see that they have prepared for the session, have planned out what they want to say, how they want to say it, and are able to run through that with me, in a practice session.

CLOSING THE SESSION

When you close a session, ask for the person's commitment by guiding the individual through a process to confirm they understand what is being asked of them. The learning continuum extends from initially acknowledging the concept has been heard, to having a full understanding of the concept, then finishing with commitment to making agreed upon behavior changes. Make sure the person explicitly commits to implementing what was discussed.

The last part of the coaching cycle is the debrief. A lot of effort goes into preparing for a coaching call or meeting, then conducting the session, but if you don't debrief you have not closed the coaching cycle. There are many reasons to conduct a debrief within a short period of time after your initial session. It should happen at an agreed upon time, so everyone is prepared.

Having a debrief shortly after is preferable because the information and thoughts shared are still fresh in participants' minds. This closeness to the original meeting allows you to better explore their feelings about the interaction. Secondly, sense of accountability wanes over time, so if you have that big discussion on a Friday, you want to catch them on the following Monday..

Many ambitious CEOs make the mistake of holding their direct reports to unrealistic standards, and being unrealistically hard on them. When dealing with accountability, you have to focus on the difference between what was agreed to as the session's goal, and what was actually attained in terms of change. This keeps situations as objective as possible, and creates the starting point for the next coaching cycle.

The learning process can get short circuited when a CEO or leader is too hard on a subordinate or colleague for falling short of a goal. It is important to avoid being hard on people. Good coaching sessions sometimes go to waste because the debrief session was not done in a timely manner, or skipped altogether. We must do all three parts; preparation, coaching and debriefing - and be mindful all along the way!

FEEDBACK

In coaching, people struggle with the notion of feedback. I am not a big fan of praising people outside of special achievements, or times when praise is specifically warranted. If someone has acted in a way that makes them deserve recognition, they should get it, but it should be limited to special circumstances. We can't recognize or praise them just to check off a box on a review sheet. It has to be thoughtful, meaningful and specific. That a leader actually notices an achievement is what matters.

Make sure compliments are genuine and specific. Instead of saying, "Wow, you made a huge difference." Consider saying, "Wow you made a huge difference, as your team's sales numbers helped compensate for the shortfall of the rest of the company!" People need to know why they matter.

We have discussed how it is crucial to follow the coaching cycle from the point where you organize your thoughts and plan what you will say, through to the debrief. Develop this plan and make sure that you have your coaching and feedback process down to an art. Keep notes about your interactions. Reflect on what you did well, what you didn't do well, and ways you will improve in the future. You might prefer to write these details down on paper, in a journal, or build a file for relevant notes and thoughts on your laptop.

When processing your coaching sessions, try to identify at what points in your session you reached each of the three stages: acknowledgement, understanding and commitment. Make a note of when the debrief began, and what statement you used to initiate the debriefing period. It is important build a narrative around your coaching sessions, because this enriches the relationships you share with each person you coach.

How feedback is delivered, the actual language used, will influence how effective a coaching session turns out to be. The preferred form of delivery varies, and communication skills will be based on a combination of maturity and individual personality. Extroverts sometimes like it direct. Other extroverts want to talk about the subject matter for a while, before receiving the direct guidance or feedback part of the coaching session.

Introverts sometimes need critiques to be gentle, while others want you to be direct. When dealing with introverts who are linear thinkers, back up your thoughts with facts, rather than spouting opinions. In some cases, extroverts who are linear thinkers also appreciate fact-driven feedback.

A final aspect of good feedback delivery is to consider whether feedback is framed in a positive or negative light. The ideal feedback balance is to start at two positive pieces of feedback for every one piece of constructive feedback. Many ambitious CEOs only deliver constructive criticism, and a gentler CEO might dispense 50/50.

I used to be a coach who had little positive feedback to give, and focused on being constructive only. I learned over time that providing positives are just as important as concentrating on areas that need improvement. Your most inexpensive incentive tool for getting people to work smarter, harder and better is sometimes a piece of thoughtful positive feedback.

ENCOURAGEMENT

The marathon brought out in me a sense of gratefulness. I am forever grateful for the encouragement I was given when I hit the wall. If not for the encouragement from the spectators, other runners, and particularly Jen and Joe in those last six miles, it would have been a far more painful and miserable experience.

Encouragement is an important aspect of giving feedback. Praise is nice, but it can be preferable to offer encouragement. This prepares others for managing the challenges that might come their way by letting them know they are smart, strong and capable. Tell them why you know they can do it. Provide encouragement that is relevant to current goals. Reassurance can feel like a glass of water in the desert.

Alternatively, giving someone praise for past achievements and using those to reference current abilities doesn't always help with preparing for immediate concerns. For example, telling me I can run a marathon today because I was successful in running half marathons during previous years seems nice, but a lot changes in our hearts, bodies and minds in just a few years' time.

Telling me that I can run five more miles today, because I ran 45 each week for the last three or four months, exemplifies encouragement. It reminds me of the commitment I made for the race, and how hard I've been working during the present time to prepare for it. One statement is based on praising the past while the other makes a valid, quantitative statement about what is occurring right now.

ACCOUNTABILITY PITFALLS, COACHING CHRONIC ISSUES AND ASSOCIATED TOOLS

The funny thing about accountability is that most people get it wrong, by thinking that it's all about how you finish, or how you hold someone accountable after a significant event has concluded. An example is, "He missed his goal, so I had to hold him accountable." The irony is people miss goals because they weren't held accountable at the right points, or because they were unclear about what was expected from them.

We need to focus on understanding their goals and making sure their goals are aligned with ours, so we are in a much better position to hold them accountable. If they fall short, accountability simply means showing them the difference between what they set out to do, and what they actually did. Don't make it personal or negative. While it may be painful to face one's failures, if they care about the goal, they will diligently work at closing the gap over time, with the help of your consistent guidance.

When coaching someone about an issue or skill that needs improvement, some coaching tools will help you work together to overcome challenges, to grow, or resolve conflicts. The first tool we will discuss is the *mirror of accountability* and how it comes in handy. Think of your left hand as a representation of a person's desire, and your right hand as a representation of their behavior. Are desire and behavior aligned? Would you place your hands together in order to show the alignment, or keep them apart because desire does not match behavior?

As the coach, move the hands closer or father apart to represent a disconnect. A CEO might be committed to the growth of the company, yet hasn't invested money in developing the senior management team. In this situation, desire does not match up with behavior. If someone is committed to running a marathon and they haven't been training, then behavior is not consistent with desire.

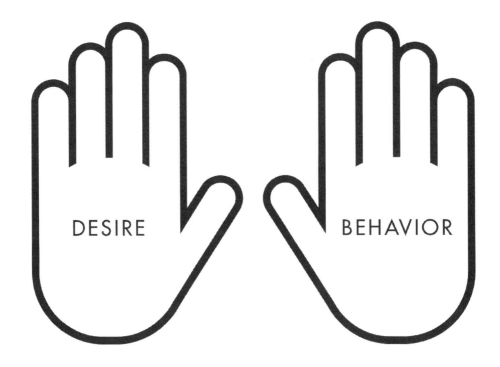

DESIRE   BEHAVIOR

Accountability is the act of helping someone understand the difference between what their goal was and what took place. Juxtaposing desire and behavior is important, so participants can agree when they see the same difference. When they see a hand, symbolizing desire, that does not align with a hand symbolizing behavior, then they have no choice but to commit to making adjustments, or come up with an alternative plan. What clicks for most people is the visual learning aspect of this exercise. If I described these ideas verbally, the match between desire and behavior would be difficult for some people to envision mentally. Once you make it into a visual exercise, the hands as symbols helps people make choices and see how the two elements might not be aligned and possibly even far apart.

ROLE OF MOTIVATION

In his book, *Drive*, NY Times best-selling author, Dan Pink, calls attention to intrinsic motivation. Intrinsic motivation is skills mastery, purpose, and autonomy. Extrinsic motivation is money, power, and recognition. Dan Pink has been an amazing mentor and all of his works have provided great learning and inspiration.

Understanding what sort of motivation drives employees, co-workers, and loved ones can help you determine how best to motivate them during a coaching situation. Are they intrinsically or extrinsically motivated? Should they work hard at improving at their job for financial reasons? Should they work hard because it will bring them greater autonomy?

Whether one is intrinsically or extrinsically motivated is a starting point for understanding how to motivate people, but let's take a different perspective. You could view it from a very basic perspective, like the hierarchy of need. Hierarchy of need represents how people are drawn toward pleasurable circumstances, and away from painful ones. Most people are aware of this but don't factor it in when they attempt to coach others. For example, will an individual work hard to hit their goal, because hitting the goal brings them pleasure? Or will they work hard to avoid missing the goal, as failure is painful?

People can be motivated by either pursuit of pleasure, or avoidance of pain. To be a great coach, you have to understand which consequence motivates the individuals you interact with most. Are you the type of person who is going to move towards winning? Or are you the type of person who doesn't want to lose?

When coaching and giving feedback, it's safest to use motivation as a way of connecting with individuals. Some people grow up in an environment with mentors and role models who were proponents of negative reinforcement. An example of this toxic technique is insulting a person when they fail at a task, so they will respond strongly to the put down by changing behaviors. I am not a fan of negative reinforcement, and I found positive reinforcement works for 90-95 percent of people.

By no means do I pretend that it works with everyone. There are people for whom negative reinforcement is a comfortable and productive means of receiving coaching. For the vast majority of people, however, it is not the best choice.

COACHING FOR REAL COMMITMENT

Earlier in the book, we talked about the difference between real and conditional commitment. As a coach, you will have to help people beyond conditional commitment. If you think a person you are coaching is guilty of conditional commitment, but they insist they are fully committed, one of the tools that we use is the *Commitment Wrecking Ball*. The Commitment Wrecking Ball metaphorically challenges one's commitment. It is easy to claim commitment but hard to prove, so citing behavior that supports commitment will either affirm or discredit their claims. This exercise asks questions about what types of behaviors they've shown to prove their focus.

Start by asking your participant to identify recent behaviors that show commitment to their spouse, children or family members. Since these are the people we see most often and care most about, it's often easy for people to think of kind, devoted acts they have done to benefit their families. Shift your questioning to work-related topics where you think commitment is lagging, and ask if they can give a comparable example of commitment. The wrecking ball sounds a lot worse than it really is. Challenging others in constructive ways can lead to meaningful conversations.

The strategy of a great coach is to listen first, then lead with questions. Smart coaching stimulates questions such as:

* "Are my employees committed enough to reach that next level?"
* "Is the COO prepared to do whatever it takes to be promoted to CEO when the current one retires?"
* "Is the CEO of this 50 million dollar company willing to do whatever it takes to get to 100 million?"
* "I'm a successful CEO, but am I committed to find a different work plus life equation when I start a family later in life?

These are all great questions that a coach or support team member should ask. Great coaches need to feel comfortable discussing commitment.

COACHING TOOL FOR OVERCONFIDENCE

A dagger is only useful at close range. Every so often, commitment can turn into overconfidence. In some cases it is difficult to coach for over-confidence, before an employee or loved one makes a mistake. It is only after you have recognized the overconfidence that you can effectively coach to it. A **_Dagger of Doubt_** is a tool for an Endurance Executive/Leader/Coach to help work through a coaching scenario where over-confidence might be at play. This exercise does not involve the direct challenge that you saw addressed in the Commitment Wrecking Ball, but it does call into question one's confidence level.

Questions to ask when checking for overconfidence during a coaching session:

* How are you so sure about this decision?

* What if you are wrong?
* What is the risk of being wrong?

We all have moments of overconfidence, and believing we are too capable can be just as detrimental as believing we aren't capable enough. The Dagger of Doubt, as a coaching tool should be used responsibly. It is a series of questions meant to make the person you are coaching seriously consider their practical skills, abilities, or whether they have the resources they need to take on a large project.

When the person who is being coached finishes considering the answers to the Dagger of Doubt questions, and concludes. "I don't have any proof. I don't have any guarantees," or I'm not so sure," they may decide their goals were impractical, or unrealistic. The Dagger of Doubt allows people to consider perspectives that their overconfidence might otherwise cancel out.

Getting the best performance possible out of an employee can seem like a battle. You have to be creative. Daggers sting, to say the least, so it is okay if the questions sting as well, but it shouldn't feel like the full brunt of a direct challenge. Some people do not respond well to direct challenges, so you have to take care when you use doubt as a tool to get an individual to soften their position.

Being a successful endurance executive, leader, or coach, means being committed to holding out the longest, even when we are mentally and physically exhausted. If a coworker or loved one wants to go in a different direction, we have to help them refocus, and send them toward the finish line. If we're coaching a coworker and they stumble or want to quit, we have to help them back up through encouragement and positive reinforcement. It takes a lot of energy. Endurance Executives will always be the people who last the longest, often under the most mental, physical, and emotional stress, to make it through the race.

CHAPTER 10 SUMMARY

When we seek to help others learn and grow, we also grow and mature emotionally. The insights we share with others also help us to see important aspects of our own personalities, strengths, and weaknesses.

An Endurance Executive understands that great coaching has three important parts: preparation, conducting a good coaching session, and a follow-up debrief.

In the case of preparation, an Endurance Executive needs to be clear if they are coaching a skill issue or a conceptual issue. They also have to be prepared to go through the key parts of a good coaching session:

* Invitation to be coached
* Roadblock review
* Leveraging motivation
* Coaching on the skill area
* Validating understanding
* Gaining commitment

CLOSING THE SESSION

This area is highlighted because it is often missed by most CEOs and other leaders. They mistake understanding for commitment. It is critical to get explicit commitment to improve.

FEEDBACK

Another area where CEOs and other leaders get wrong in coaching is feedback. They don't consider the impact of how they articulate feedback and the impact it will have on the learner. Too much praise can cause a learner to focus on that and not on the area that requires improvement. Too much constructive criticism will demoralize someone from improving in the required area.

ENCOURAGEMENT

This tool is not leveraged enough by CEOs and other leaders in my experience. Encouraging people helps them to focus going forward on what they have to accomplish and in many cases improve.

ACCOUNTABILITY PITFALLS, COACHING CHRONIC ISSUES AND ASSOCIATED TOOLS

The funny thing about accountability is that most people get it wrong, by thinking that it's all about how you finish, or how you hold someone accountable after a significant event has concluded. However, accountability starts with alignment at the beginning.

Coaching chronic issues are difficult but using a mirror of accountability can show the disconnect between someone's desire and behavior.

ROLE OF MOTIVATION

An Endurance Executive understands what motivates the person they are coaching. This motivation is needed to help the learner navigate uncomfortable periods of getting coached and trying to improve in a certain area.

COACHING FOR REAL COMMITMENT

In some coaching cases, a learner might insist they are committed even though their performance indicates otherwise. A tool called the "commitment wrecking ball" is a tactic of directly challenging someone's commitment by asking for behavioral proof of commitment. If the learner continues to insist they are committed even though they are unable to give proof, compare their commitment to the goal in question to their commitment outside of work to a family member.

COACHING TOOL FOR OVERCONFIDENCE

Every so often, commitment can turn into overconfidence. In some cases, it is difficult to coach for overconfidence before an employee or loved one makes a mistake. The dagger of doubt is a tactic to introduce doubt by questioning a learner's certainty about their overconfidence. Can they deliver proof that their overconfidence is warranted? In most cases this will begin lowering the overconfidence because they stop to think about what is driving their certainty.

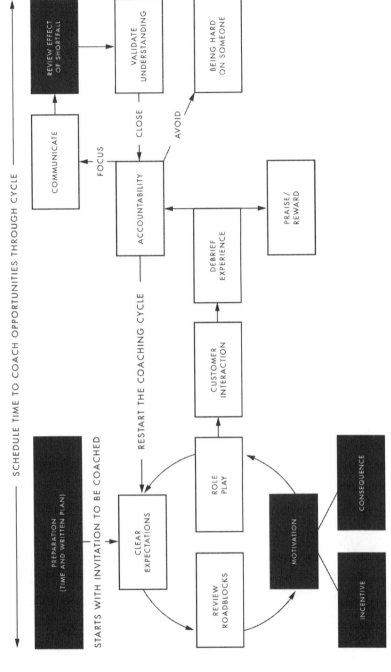

COACHING CYCLE

SCHEDULE TIME TO COACH OPPORTUNITIES THROUGH CYCLE

REFLECTIONS:

1. If you have tried to coach someone, would the outcome have been different if you invested more time in preparation?
2. Would the result have been different if you were more organized and had a specific method? How would it be different, and with whom? We want you to visualize with whom you could have made a difference.
3. When you've coached someone who has fallen short of meeting their goals, did you walk them through the process of acknowledging their challenges? Did they understand what was expected of them, as well as the shortcomings of the situation? Did they commit to changing their behavior?
4. When I get feedback, do I pay attention to the ratio of positive to negative?
5. Do I consistently encourage my direct reports?

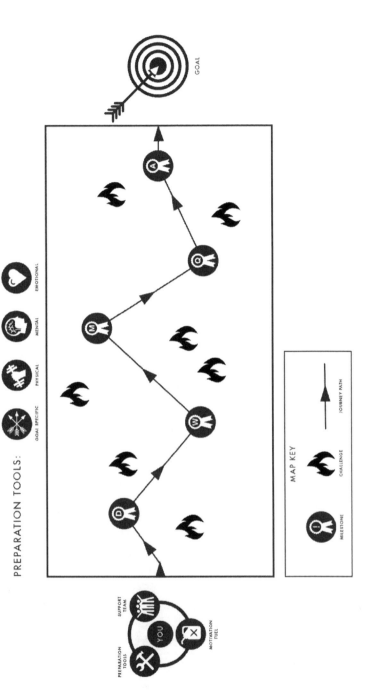

JOURNEY MAP:

CONCLUSION: WHAT NOW?

The last quarter mile of the Marine Corps Marathon was uphill. Having suffered for the better part of 12 miles, it seemed fitting that the last quarter mile would be the ultimate test of my resolve. While it was painful, I was able to run up the hill. Crossing the finish line was an amazing feeling, in spite of the pain.

I got my medal, said my goodbyes to the other runners who'd supported me, and started looking for my family so we could celebrate. It was great to see my wife, kids, and others who came out to support me. Our celebration was short and sweet; I wanted to go home, lay down, stretch and rest. Over the next couple of weeks, I celebrated with all of the different people who supported me in preparing for the race.

Writing this book is, in some regards, my final and most fulfilling celebration. This book has been a journey. Prior to the race, I was aware of all of these concepts. I later began to develop these ideas found in this book. While I thought I was doing a decent job of living the principles of an Endurance Executive, "hitting the wall" served as a reality check. Like most people, I still had room to grow.

The race experience helped me take concepts I had worked on since my days as a CEO of a wine company, find the language with which to discuss them, and compile them into a useful guidebook. Hitting the wall at mile 14 wasn't my intended goal, but persevering through the remainder of the race provided insights and revelations that inspired me to capture my story.

The concept of the Endurance Executive is built around the training required to make it through the bigger races that are ahead of us—the long, often rugged, road that makes up our work and private lives. Even those who are not in the business world, or for whom home and family hold primary focus, must strive always toward performance improvement, as parents, as friends, spouses and community members.

Becoming an Endurance Executive is as much about having the right mindset to overcome life's hurdles life as it is about becoming an ambitious business leader. Depending on where you are in your career, whatever that career might be, you will be able to appreciate and apply ideas from this book into your professional and personal development.

LIFE'S THE LONGER RACE WE'RE ALL RUNNING

This book started with the concept of endurance and the question, "What race are you running?" In my case, I wasn't just a marathoner and athlete; I was running in a much bigger race, given my other ambitious goals.

The experience helped me realize that I would love to help others ask themselves the introspective questions that nurture growth and life-long mental (and physical) fitness. I wanted to help CEOs and leaders begin an introspective journey.

Whether you have to persevere through a metaphorical wall, or go after an ambitious set of goals, it is important to understand the different components of your motivation fuel: passion, desire and commitment. All three are unique and I hope after reading this book, you have a better understanding of e Nowach.

If you prepare for all the challenges ahead, you increase the probability of success. Break preparation down into four sub-groups: goal-specific, mental, emotional and physical. Rigorous planning is required for any large achievement.

Never forget the power of your support team. I have always had one, but after my race, I saw that I needed a much larger network of people filling different support roles in my life. I knew I had to empower them to give me feedback, encouragement, and most importantly, hold me accountable. Success is not a solitary pursuit. It's a team effort.

So many people out there have a passion for helping others. People wake up in the morning and they want to make a difference, to be a part of something. When we think about endurance CEOs and endurance executives, they don't just receive support, but also provide it to others. Strong coaching strategies provide a way that everyone can help, while continuing your own learning journey.

WHAT RACE ARE YOU RUNNING?

Hitting the wall, and picking ourselves back up again, will help us learn to manage our goals differently. We must become aware of our goals, understand their significance in building a self-actualized life. Instead of just holding these goals in our minds, out of immediate sight, commit to writing goals on paper, and share goals with others.

These ideas aren't new. Similar concepts have been explored in different ways, in numerous books throughout the past thirty years. But, hopefully this anecdote will inspire you to document your goals with our goal matrix, juxtaposing personal goals with family and business goals.

While using the tools in this book, if you find you've fallen short, you will be able to gain a new sense of perspective to ensure your goals are congruent, realistic and don't compete with each another for time and energy.

Focus on conservation versus consumption as a primary part of goal achievement. Consume when you must, but do so with wisdom and awareness. In past years, I lived for the moment, but this trait does not match up to the principles of the Endurance Executive.

The Endurance Executive goes into the race with eyes open, and their minds sharp in knowing that some of the most important resources take time to renew. When we are out on the racecourse, with miles left to go and many hills ahead, conservation will keep us fueled for our journeys.

What race are you running? Do you think you've done a good job preparing for that race? Are you preparing to merely run, or are you preparing to win? If you're preparing to win, look at your goals and what kind you need to set. What kind of support team do you have? If you are committed to living a better life, making a difference, and winning, then your goals are already clear. They are just waiting to be written down, with your preparation plan in place and your support team at your side.

When my daughter asked me, "So dad, are you going to run another marathon?" The answer is simple. "Absolutely."

The measure of a marathon experience is a little bit about running a time, and a whole lot about what you learn from it. You might not feel you ran the fastest race, but when you learn as much as I did, you feel like the winner.

Pick your race. Know your race. Prepare to win.

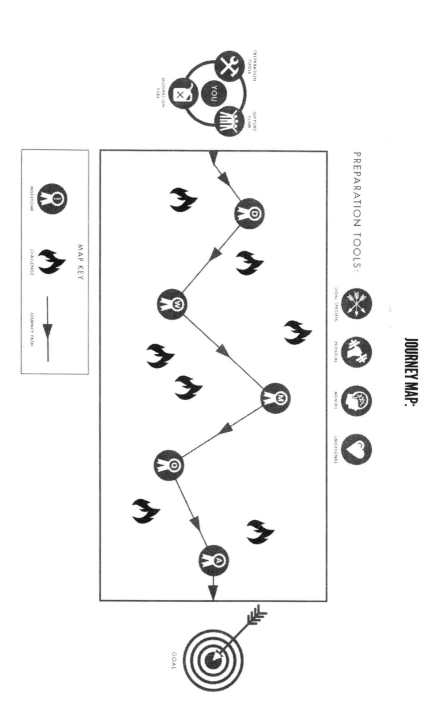

JOURNEY MAP:

PREPARATION TOOLS:

GOAL-SPECIFIC

PHYSICAL

MENTAL

EMOTIONAL

PREPARATION TOOLS

MOTIVATION FUEL

YOU

SUPPORT TEAM

MAP KEY

MILESTONE

CHALLENGE

JOURNEY PATH

GOAL

Get In Touch

T: (703)348-6451

Email: alex@enduranceexec.com

Web: www.enduranceexec.com

GLOSSARY

Accountability Loop: A term for a check and balance around a goal that helps individuals stay focused on the initial goal by having a 3rd party like a support team member check on progress towards the initial goal.

Adaptability (self-regulation): A sub-component of the emotional intelligence term of self- regulation. The term refers to a person's ability to adjust to a given situation.

Commitment Wrecking Ball: A tool used to challenge one's commitment by challenging someone's commitment in a direct way by highlighting behavior that isn't consistent with the commitment. The purpose of the challenge is to affirm or discredit ones claims of commitment.

Conditional Commitments: The term means that someone is willing to commit to a goal but under certain conditions. When someone will only commit to a goal under conditions, the commitment is conditional.

Conscientiousness (self-regulation): A sub-component of the emotional intelligence term of self- regulation. The term refers to the ability to be thoughtful of other people and elements around them.

Conservation Mindset: a mindset that is focused on getting individuals to pay closer attention to their time, energy and other key resources to pursuit personal, family, and professional goals.

Counterintuitive Thinking: Challenging generally accepted thinking or practices to increase potential for positive outcomes.

Dagger of Doubt: A coaching tool used to help a person challenge a belief or a position of over confidence that will work against them. It involves asking a person how did the individual arrive at being so sure of a position. It is based on that no one is 100% sure if anything and agrees that it is possible that there can be an alternative to their position and/or belief. From this point the coach has introduced doubt into a coaching situation which can be used to move someone point of view.

Debrief: The final phase of the coaching cycle where the person being coached reviews with their coach what the person being coached was able to accomplish and where the person fell short on the agreed upon items in their initial coaching session.

De-escalating Tension: Purposeful moments in the day to manage and reduce stress

Discipline (self-regulation): A sub-component of the emotional intelligence term of self- regulation. The term refers to a person's ability to exert self control and keep impulsivity to a minimum. Individuals have varying degrees of this on a natural basis and contrary to popular belief can develop this area by being more thoughtful in terms of where the individual invests their energy and self-control to exhibit restraint.

Drive-by Coaching: Ad-hoc coaching that is impulsive, unexpected, and very re-active.

Extrinsic Motivation: Motivations that come from external factors like money, power, and recognition.

Goal-Specific Preparation: A type of preparation that is aligned around a specific goal. If someone goal is to work abroad in a foreign country where the individual doesn't speak the primary language, a goal specific preparation would be to learn the primary language even though it might not be an obligatory requirement.

Interplay: How two elements can play off one another like desire and commitment. You cannot be successful with just one and need both to interplay with one another.

Intrinsic Motivation: Motivations that come from within the individual. Examples are skills mastery, purpose, and autonomy.

Logging Miles: The act an endurance athlete uses to track their workouts, training, and runs to ensure they are meeting expectations and necessary mileage

Managed Up: The act of managing someone who you report to that needs direction from below on a matter or topic that generally they are not familiar with so they rely on a direct report to manage up and guide him or her on what they should do.

Mental Preparation: Organizing one's thoughts in preparation to act on processes that will enable them to execute as planned and if things don't go as planned problem solve to arrive to the best outcome.

Mental Preparation Loop: The act of reflecting back on a day where you prepared for a specific event in the morning and looking back on it to see if the right preparation was taken. Were the right decisions made or acted upon? What else could have been done to maximize the outcome?

Mirror of Accountability: A tool used in coaching for accountability that is meant to juxtapose when desire and behaviors are not aligned. A coach uses his/her hands to symbolize desire on one side and behavior on the other size and show how they are not aligned and can be positioned as far apart as the coach wants, for effect in trying to drive a point home.

Peer Executive Group: A formal group of executive peers, who share experiences, offer advice, and hold each other accountable to hit personal, family and business goals. The group is made up of both internal and external peers, and can also be called a Peer Executive Forum.

Random Learning: Learning from time to time that does not sustain continuous upward growth in a particular area and lacking in overall purpose.

Reflection: To look back on a moment, situation or longer period of time, and review the events that took place, decisions that affected the outcomes, as well as emotions and other key factors.

Self Actualizing Pursuits: Activities that create fulfillment because of the passion associated with the pursuit and the happiness and fulfillment derived from the activity.

Self Awareness: The ability for one to look inward and understand emotions, perceptions, thoughts, and beliefs

Self Talk: Having positive, or negative, conversations with oneself to prepare for an event or solving a problem

Self-actualization: The desire for self-fulfillment and/or realizing one's full potential

Self-regulation: A sub-component of the emotional intelligence that is comprised of 4 sub-components: self-control, trust, adaptability and conscientiousness. This area is also referred to the soft skills area of self-management so an individual can continue to operate at a high level in complex environments like rapid growth or managing conflict.

The Edge: A term referred to the limit at which an individual can go no further prior to reaching the wall. It is said that to really understand the limits of where the edge is, an endurance executive has to go past the edge.

The Wall: a running term used to describe the point at which your body is no longer able to process the lactic acid produced by your muscles during extreme exertion. In business terms, it describes a point one reaches in a career where upward movement and growth is stunted; career exhaustion sets in and someone's happiness starts to decline.

Trust (self-regulation): A sub-component of the emotional intelligence term "self- regulation." The term refers to a person's ability to believe in someone else that they will honor what they have said they would do in a given situation.

Tuning In Empathetically: This refers to the ability of an individual to listen to a 3rd person in an attempt to try to feel the same way the 3rd person might be feeling based on what the individual is listening to and seeing in the 3rd person they are trying to be empathetic towards.

ACKNOWLEDGEMENTS

This book, much like the marathon that inspired it, was a challenging and rewarding journey that I could not have fully traversed without an amazing support team. It was made possible only through a number of significant contributions from those in my closest circle of support

At the top of that list is my wonderful wife, Mary. She supported me through long hours of absence caused by training for multiple marathons, operating a busy consulting firm, and the writing of this book over the last 2+ years. Right with her in terms of encouragement are my 3 children, Lily, Jack and Leo. They each had my back in their own way not even realizing how their presence, interactions with me and general quality family time impacted me—and this book.

I was fortunate that my brother, Erik, had an uncanny ability to chime in from afar when I needed some humor or encouragement as I dove deeply into the creation of Endurance Executive. I am very thankful for the role models in my life, my dad, Alfredo, and my loving mother, Liliana. It's a bittersweet feeling to know that my mother, who passed nearly 15 years ago, was not here to see the book come to fruition. She epitomized many aspects of an Endurance Executive later in life as she battled cancer.

On the competitive running end of the spectrum, I have to first thank my great friend, Matt Moser, for getting me hooked on running. An accomplished runner who finished multiple 50 mile marathons and ultra-marathons, he started me off small with my first 10k race and the rest is history. Another great supporter is my lawyer and friend, Eric Horvitz, who also encouraged me to run farther and push myself. He is trying to convince me to join him doing triathlons, but I am not sure I will go that far. I also must thank my marathon training comrades from the Metro Run & Walk running group in Springfield, Va.—and in particular, my sage coach, Bruce Whitson: Your stories are amazing and I appreciate the insight you have shared with me over the last 2+ years.

One of the concepts of Endurance Executive is to always recruit great members to your support team. My 2 peer accountability partners, Mike Carroll and Frederic Lucas, who run business similar to mine, have provided amazing support by challenging me to grow and push myself. These two men, based in Milwaukee and Montreal respectively, have been instrumental in the growth of my business through calls on a monthly basis for more than 3 years. They gave me positive affirmation in droves through the ambitious endeavor of writing a book while managing my personal life, family and business.

I would be remiss if I didn't thank a couple of my business mentors, Andy Miller and Dave Kurlan, who have provided great vision and wisdom to me in many aspects of my journey, including the creation of Endurance Executive. Andy has been a friend and mentor for the last 11 years. An accomplished weight lifter and tremendously fit executive, Andy was a great sounding board for many of my ideas from the book. Dave runs two companies, Objective Management Group and Dave Kurlan & Associates and still finds time to coach me on being an elite sales consultant and holding me accountable to my goals. Dave also helped me with inspiring words of encouragement as I experienced my own "wall" of writer's block.

In the book I mention the importance of peer executive forums. I am grateful to my former Entrepreneurs' Organization forum mates. Mark R: your unique perspective of a thoughtful mad genius helped me get unstuck with writer's block a couple of times. Tim T: your enthusiasm and overall positivity helped out on many occasions. Greg D: Thank you for keeping me on my toes and always challenging me with various Endurance Executive concepts. Yoav: although infrequent, our chats and time together were always well timed and infused me with the positive energy to continue writing the book. David E: Thank you for being a great client and for inspiring me to write my book as I watched your own book-writing journey. Darryl: I know I was always able to count on you for good humor and encouragement when the progress of the book slowed to a crawl.

As I look back on my 30 month book-writing journey, I have a worked with a number of clients who have unknowingly made an impact on my business as well as this book. None more than my friends at Acumen Solutions and Dataprise who challenged me as much as I have challenged each company as their advisor, coach and consultant to realize their best.

As this book came together, I have to thank my amazing graphic designer, Jeff Breidenbach, who is responsible for the cover and branding around Endurance Executive.

Finally, I have to thank my editor, Jason Carpenter. He has his own story and journey that is inspiring on its own and I was very lucky to have a guide on what can seem like a lonely journey—and helped to push me past the finish line.

Get In Touch

T: (703)348-6451

Email: alex@enduranceexec.com

Web: www.enduranceexec.com

51545616R00114

Made in the USA
Charleston, SC
25 January 2016